J. McCowan

# A Tour in Canada

J. McCowan

**A Tour in Canada**

ISBN/EAN: 9783337327620

Printed in Europe, USA, Canada, Australia, Japan

Cover: Foto ©Andreas Hilbeck / pixelio.de

More available books at **www.hansebooks.com**

# A TOUR IN CANADA

By Rev. J. M'COWAN,
CROMDALE.

---

REPRINTED FROM "ELGIN COURANT AND COURIER."

---

1894.

# PREFACE.

*THE following appeared in the form of articles in the "Elgin Courant and Courier," and, as some of my friends desired to have the whole in a connected book form, the Editor very kindly agreed to throw off a few copies from the newspaper type. This, and the fact that I might thus have a memento of a most pleasant trip, accounts for the appearance of the book. I had also the hope that the information it furnishes with regard to the country might be useful to intending colonists or tourists.*

*I wish here also to acknowledge in a sentece then extreme kindness and generous hospitality which I experienced on all hands, and which was specially extended to me by certain of the public gentlemen, notably so by Sir Donald A. Smith, of Montreal.*

*J. M'COWAN.*

*Cromdale Manse,*
*July, 1894.*

# A TOUR IN CANADA.

IT had been my desire for years to visit America and witness some of the wonders of the New World for myself, but matters of a personal character, and more imperative in their claims than pleasure-seeking, always interfered. During last winter, however, it was my fortune to hear ex-Bailie Stuart, of Inverness, deliver one of his racy lectures on Canada, and while listening to it my old ambition became so intensified that I resolved, if possible, to give effect to it in course of the year by crossing the Atlantic. I communicated my resolution to some friends, who encouraged the proposal by offering to occupy my pulpit in my absence. Thus every barrier was removed, and to the clergymen who assisted me I shall ever owe a debt of sincere gratitude for their valuable services which relieved me for ten Sundays, and enabled me to see and to gain an insight into American life, character, and scenery, which was profitable to myself, and which I hope to be able to make useful to others. The route selected was from Liverpool to Montreal. A short run on the electric railway along the south bank of the river Mersey brought me to the platform nearest the dock where the Royal Mail Steamship Parisian —the finest of the fleet of floating palaces owned by the celebrated Allan Line Company—was busy taking on board passengers, luggage, and cargo. There was great excitement on the pier, cabbies and porters shouting and hurrying to and fro. The crowd was so dense that no small energy and courage was necessary to push one's way to the gangway which was closely besieged. Half-an-hour was lost before my luggage was safely deposited in the state-room, and the porter, considerably relieved, in return for a tip, respectfully touched his cap and disappeared. After a general survey of the saloon I took up a position on the upper deck, which commanded a complete view of the crowd on the wharf and about the gangway. It was interesting to notice the scenes presented by the different groups, and to listen to the wise counsels and last good-byes that were being exchanged below. But withal there was a feeling of intense novelty, almost of amusement, in the scene to one who was neither alarmed about his own affairs nor weighed down with the cares of others. The clang of the bell at last announced that all was ready for starting—the gangway was hauled ashore, the moorings let off, and the Parisian slowly steamed down the river, and out into the Atlantic. The weather was beautiful, the sun shining out brilliantly, the sea calm as glass, and everything giving promise of a most enjoyable and pleasant voyage. In about a couple of hours the passengers got fairly settled down, half acquainted with each other. I failed to recognise more than one individual out of over two hundred saloon passengers. I accosted him by name, but in the course of conversation it became evident that he did not recognise me, for on being asked if there were any other passengers on board hailing from the beautiful strath to which he belonged, he replied, yes, there is one, mentioning my full name and address, but added, I have not seen him as yet ! I at once changed the conversation, and left my friend to find me out for himself, which he succeeded in doing before we reached Montreal. To account for the difficulty, it may be stated that I was dressed as a layman, but the change of garb being got over, and the mutual recognitions being gone through, we enjoyed each other's company as far as Toronto. At our first dinner everybody had a glance at those who were to be their fellow-passengers for the next eight or nine days ; and if an opinion may be expressed after a day at sea, the general impression was that it would be difficult to bring together a nicer lot of people. Among them were Sir John Thomson, Prime Minister of Canada, returning from the gay capital of France, where he had been acting as one of the British arbitrators on the Behring Sea question ; Sir Charles and Lady Tupper, with their son, the Honourable C. H. Tupper, the energetic young Minister of Marine and Fisheries, Mr Douglas, Private Secretary to the Prime Minister, and six delegates chosen from among the practical farmers of the United Kingdom—three being English, two Scotch, and one Irish. The notabilities of the saloon were rather a mixed community. Military talent was represented by General Simpson; science and literature, by Professor M'Lellan and a Cambridge don; medicine, by a Scotch, a Canadian, and an Irish doctor; law, by an English barrister and a solicitor from Chicago; divinity in its different forms was ably supported by more than a dozen clergymen of different denominations. There were Canadian statesmen, a millionaire, an eccentric Jew, a "corporate" Hollander, and several gallant (?) American Colonels, &c., &c.

On board ship one comes in contact with men of every profession and of the most varied attainments, with men who have risen from the ranks by their own ability and energy to positions of honour, trust, and independence, as well as with men who have been born great, all bent on finding a wider scope in the New World for the hampered and restricted sphere they were condemned to at home. But on board there are no society restrictions, and any drawback to a free exchange of sentiment between the passengers must be generally attributed to the state of the weather, which has a much more degenerating influence on the individual passenger than the restricted laws of sociality. The weather acts upon the ocean, the ocean upon the ship, and the ship upon the most of its inhabitants, and so, according to Newton's "laws of nature," there is necessarily a reaction for every action, so in this case the reaction occurs, and it is a matter of regret that it develops into jealousy, hatred, and suspicion with regard to the party who has resisted or succumbed to that disastrous epidemic which rages among those who have not gained their sea legs and their sea stomachs—that *mal de mer* which one of the steerage passengers rendered into intelligible language by stating "It was jest puttin' yer han' doon yer throat an' pu'in yer stomach up, an' houldin' it ticht in yer haun before yer een." But, as the fates would have it, our passage was extremely good, and after a couple of days' experience on the dark blue sea there was no necessity for resorting to such disagreeable measures for relieving the feelings.

The Parisian sailed into Lough Foyle early on the second morning, and we had a prospect of old Ireland, which looked as fair and as green as it is represented to look. Here the steamer remained at anchor off Moville till the mails arrived, and were placed on board about two o'clock on Friday afternoon. In the interval many passengers went ashore in small sailing crafts, and had their first experience on an Irish jaunting car by a drive to Green Castle. Here Sir John Thompson and the Hon. C. H. Tupper met Colonel Stevenson, who was spending a few weeks in the neighbourhood, and there renewed a pleasant acquaintanceship which they had formed in Canada a few years before. About three o'clock in the afternoon the powerful engines of the Parisian were again in motion, the propeller started its revolutions, and soon the noble ship was ploughing the broad Atlantic and sailing straight into the setting sun. Towards dusk land faded from our view, the ground swell began to rise, and the vessel to roll. The dinner table was not so crowded, and, indeed, before bedtime two-thirds of the passengers were busily engaged "feeding the whales," as the phrase goes! Standing alone on the deck, and under circumstances calculated to stimulate thought, a variety of subjects for contemplation rose before my mind. Before us, in whatever direction the eye might roam, spread "old ocean's grey and melancholy waste," inviting serious reflection on its vastness—the perils associated with its navigation, and the capabilities of human ingenuity in conducting such wonderful and speedy communication over its bosom between the Old and the New World. On Sunday, according to a standing rule, divine service was conducted on board, after the form of the Church of England. It is difficult to imagine anything more impressive and solemn than a religious service at sea. Isolated from the rest of the world as effectually, for the time being, as if we belonged to a different sphere; tossed about on the wide expanse of the mighty ocean, far away from the familiar sound of the church bells—to feel that even here He who holds the waters in the hollow of His hand, and who directs the planets in their courses, that we are able to unite in prayer, praise, and adoration of the Great Creator with all our fellow-Christians throughout the world—that here, even, we may carry in thought to the throne of grace all who are nearest and dearest to us, though in the body we are far away from them. Here we are bound by the ties of a common, a truly spiritual, religion. How appropriate the singing of the hymn—

> Lord, whom winds and seas obey,
> Guide us through our watery way ;
> In the hollow of Thy hand
> Hide and bring us safe to land.

At the close of the service a collection was made in aid of the Mariner's Orphanage, at Liverpool. It amounted to over five pounds. A concert for the same purpose realised some twenty-three pounds, and, including intermediate and steerage, a total sum of thirty-five pounds was raised. Sir Charles Tupper presided at the concert, and paid a deservedly high compliment to the captain and the officers of the Parisian for their attention and courtesy. He also referred to the splendid qualities of the ship. Sir John Thompson moved a vote of thanks to the Chairman and all concerned, ending with a warm eulogy on Captain Ritchie, remarking upon his popularity and attention to duty, praise which was most enthusiastically applauded by the audience. An exhibition of Canadian lime-light views was given by Mr Mills, a Welsh artist. The entertainment was most instructive, and heartily appreciated by all. But, perhaps, the most enjoyable evening to all of us, as far as I could judge, was spent in dancing on deck, an amusement in which nearly all the passengers joined. Among the many means of affording exercise and sources of amusement were quoits, skittles, chess, draughts, whist, euchre, &c., &c. Some of the passengers, comfortably wrapped with rugs, lounged on deck chairs, and read almost the whole day long, the meal-bell alone being effective in tearing them away from some interesting volume, lent from the ship's library. Promenading the deck was a most popular and delightful mode of taking exercise when the weather was favourable. The smoking-room was the favourite resort of all lovers of the weed, and of all who wished to indulge in the games of whist and euchre.

Early one morning the wonders of the great deep appeared quite close to us in the shape of a flock, or what the nautical man would call "a school," of whales spouting and rolling over, apparently in play. By mid-day of the same day land was supposed to be sighted, amidst excitement, but time proved it to be an immense iceberg. We were now apparently fairly come into the region of the icebergs, for in every direction they might be seen, varying in size from small blocks to great mountains. On a closer approach to one, which was particularly grand, it seemed to resemble a large fortification, with battlements, turrets, and walls all complete. It presented a magnificent spectacle. The darkish tint on the south side gradually disappeared as we neared it, to be replaced by rainbow colours of the most dazzling brilliancy, which wavered and sparkled like immense gems set in a mountain of silver. But the beauty of nature's transformation scenes as exhibited in the iceberg must be seen to be either enjoyed or understood. The weather while we were in this quarter was bitterly cold, though the sun shone brilliantly from an unclouded sky. After passing the icebergs land was sighted, and soon the Parisian was ploughing alongside Belle Isle, which looked to me to be very bald and barren. The only inhabitants are the lighthouse keepers, who telegraph all ships to Quebec, so that our approach was announced there a couple of days before our arrival. Passing Belle Isle the strait of the same name was sailed through, with Newfoundland on the one hand and Labrador on the other. After entering the Gulf of St Lawrence land disappeared again till the island of Anticosti was sighted. The first stop was at Rimouski, where a tender delivered and received mails and passengers. This would be about seven o'clock on Friday morning, a morning that proved to be foggy and drizzling. But it cleared up into a beautiful warm day with bright sun shining overhead. As the Gulf of the St Lawrence narrows, and as we ascend farther up the majestic river of the same name, the scenery on either bank, which is very fine, comes into view. The wood-covered hills slope gradually down to the water's edge, and here and there small white villages make their appearance. The many islands dotted all over the river give to it a most romantic appearance. As we approached Quebec the scenery becomes really splendid to look at. But the passengers were so excited with preparation for landing that few of them devoted much of their time in the enjoyment of it.

There were 661 passengers on board ; of these 201 were saloon, 172 intermediate, and 228 steerage. The majority of the latter were Scandinavians, the remainder being Scotch, English, and Irish. These all brought on board with them provision supply sufficient for the whole voyage. Though the ship's fare is everything that could be desired, somehow the food has earned a reputation which exists only in imagination. A careful study of the difference in fare and comfort between the steerage and intermediate should convince all who can possibly afford the latter to book by it. The state or bedrooms of the intermediate are exceptionally comfortable, and, except in luxurious fittings, are almost equal to the first class, while the food and attendance are but very little behind. The fare of the intermediate is seven and that of the steerage five guineas. The steerage passenger has to provide himself with mattress, blankets, and utensils for his food, and when the total sum is deducted from the intermediate fare of seven guineas the difference is so small that it is more than counterbalanced by the advantages derived. It may be mentioned that those taking money should do so by draft or in gold. But in no case should paper money be taken, as the discount on getting it exchanged is rather heavy. The purser on board exchanges money, but even he discounts paper money. Gold and silver he exchanges at par—that is without charging for the exchange ; but English gold is exchangeable all over America at par. English and American money is good on board ship, but intending emigrants should provide themselves before starting with all necessary trifles, such as ink, pen, paper, tobacco, &c.

Altogether the voyage across was most enjoyable, and will ever remain a subject for pleasant recollections and sweet memories. The latter part of it was simply delightful, and it was with genuine regret that we parted at Quebec.

## Quebec.

This fine city of 80,000 or 100,000 inhabitants spreads itself out along the base, and also occupies the summit of a lofty crag rising almost from the water edge of the St Lawrence river at a point where that river is comparatively narrow. It has thus a commanding and magnificent situation, and, from the strong fortresses and powerful battlements which protect it, may be regarded as holding the key to Canada. Its historical interest is so great, and its natural beauties so attractive, that it is impossible to describe the city except in the most general manner. My object is not so much to give detailed descriptions as to give passing glimpses sufficient to arouse the interest of the public, and to cause them to bestow a little attention upon the interests and the beauties of the New World.

As far back as 1535 the rugged cliffs of Quebec afforded shelter to the first European—Jacques Cartier—who, after braving the dangers of the deep, steered his craft up the river and landed there. The few huts thereafter erected soon developed into a settlement. Then the French fur companies, recognising its natural advantages, established it as an important trading post. As it gradually increased in commercial enterprise, the fortifications were enlarged and strengthened till Quebec became the impregnable strong-hold of Canada, and so remained for a period of 224 years, when it was taken by the English under the leadership of General Wolfe.

The lumber trade that is carried on at Quebec is enormous, consequently the river and wharves are particularly crowded and busy with the steamers and crafts of all nations; while on land the railways are equally thronged, so that on all sides are indications of a prosperous and thriving population. On landing the visitor should go direct to Cape Diamond to receive his first impressions of his surroundings. From this cape the view of the St Lawrence forms a superb panorama. An extensive range of mountain, forest, river, stream, and valley, unsurpassed in any country, stretches out before the eyes. The Lower Town is the business and commercial quarter with nothing of special interest except the irregular and narrow streets, and the ancient style of the architecture of many of the houses. Passing through this locality one feels as if he were treading on a strange and weird land. It is entirely distinct in every feature compared with the Upper Town with its substantial blocks, splendid public buildings, thriving schools, comfortable hotels, and its large and well-filled convents.

The tourist should visit the Chapel and Convent

of St Ursula, where many valuable paintings are to be seen and religiously laid up. Here, too, are deposited many holy relics; as, for example, the body of St Clement brought from the Catacombs of Rome, the supposed skull of St Justus, what purports to be a bit of the Holy Cross, and a part of the Crown of Thorns. In the English Cathedral, which is built after the Roman style of architecture, lie near the pulpit the remains of the Duke of Richmond, a Governor-General of Canada, who died in 1819, as indicated by a mural tablet on the wall. The wall is also adorned by the tattered colours of the 69th Regiment. After having seen the Basilica and the Seminary Chapel the Grand Battery should be visited. Here fifty mounted guns command the entrance to the harbour, while the out'ook on mountain and valley is very fine. The citadel is approached by the Chain and Dalhousie Gates, where the visitor is brought directly opposite the Officers' Quarters, in which Princess Louise was accommodated, and received such a cordial and enthusiastic reception.

The cemeteries are worthy of notice, especially the Protestant one on Mount Hermon, where among the many beautiful monuments there is one commemorating the sad death of the immigrants on board the burning ship Montreal.

But for extent and grandeur, perhaps, the view from the Flagstaff Bastion, which is 350 feet above water level, is unequalled. From here the mighty St Lawrence is seen in all its majesty sweeping down towards the ocean. There, too, is seen standing boldly forth in unclouded beauty the village of Beauport, the Island of Orleans, and Point Levis. To the west are the famous blood-stained Plains of Abraham, the scene of the ever-memorable battle which transferred Canada to the British Crown. On the Plains a monument has been erected with the following inscription:— "This pillar was erected by the British Army in Canada, A.D. 1849, His Excellency Lieutenant General Sir Benjamin d'Urban being commander of the forces, to replace that erected by Governor General Lord Aylmer, in 1832, which was broken and defaced, and is deposited beneath." The Falls of Montmorency, with the natural steps, should not be omitted, as the scenery about is exquisite. The St Foy and St Louis roads afford splendid drives, lined as they are on either side by

beautiful villas and handsome mansions standing
in beautifully-enclosed grounds. Here and there
the drive is through avenues of trees, graceful
elms, stately pine, and fine birch. The trees
spread their branches and foliage out across the
roadway, and form a beautiful and pleasing shade
to the passer-by. The residence and farm of
Colonel Rhodes deserve special mention. Around
this abode a perpetual summer may be said to
reign. Greenhouses, hothouses, &c., with conser-
vatories and vineries, abound. The beauty and
the intoxicating perfumes of the flowers of the
garden are most pleasing. Equally rich and
abundant are the strawberries, grapes, pears, and
oranges which are reared here to great perfection,
and also I might add at great expense.
This gentleman does not confine himself
to the cultivation of flowers and fruit alone, but
he raises cattle for breeding and show purposes.
The drive by the St Louis road is altogether most
delightful, with its cool breeze from the river tem-
pering the hottest summer air. An extended
drive to Lake Beauport and the Shrine and Falls
of St Anne will repay the sight-seer a hundredfold. The Parish Church of Beauport, erected
about three hundred years ago, was consecrated
by the Pope to St Anne. To this holy shrine
thousands of pilgrims repair—often as a penance
or in discharge of vows. The pilgrimages take
place chiefly on the 26th of July, which is the
festal day of the celebrated saint. The crowds of
pilgrims that resort thither are so large that, for
the comfortable accommodation of the worshippers, a fine church has been erected within
recent years. In the building are placed thousands of crutches, left in days gone by by those
who had departed cured of their lamenesses or
other maladies by the saint. A finger-bone of the
saint herself is supposed to be deposited, as a
sacred relic, in the sanctuary ; and on kissing it
worldly evils and misfortunes are said to vanish at
once from the devotee, while similar results are
also said to follow a steadfast gaze on the piles of
crutches. The despairing are often here filled
with new hope, while the feeble and the faint are
daily restored to health and strength.

There is not a more interesting town than
Quebec in the New World. In and around the
city almost every building, crag, and knoll is asso-

ciated with some stirring battle or siege chronicled in comparatively modern history. The French element is largely prevalent, while France's ancient laws most generally prevail. There is abundant interest to detain the tourist in this city for a week, and, after having seen all that is to be seen in the town and neighbourhood, I think he will be impressed with the thought, as I was, that no more fitting entrance to the glorious and prosperous Dominion that lies beyond it could be imagined than this beautiful, this historic, this quaint, this fairy-like, and romantic City of Quebec.

From Quebec to Montreal by steamer is a much more interesting and enjoyable journey than going by rail. The view along both banks of the noble river is beautiful in the extreme. The country generally is low and fertile, partly wooded and partly cultivated, and ever and again as the steamer ploughs her way upwards we come upon the openings of new rivers that are rolling down their waters to join the main stream. French settlements are seen to follow in close succession, nestling themselves close along the water edge. The villages are quaint, clean looking, and picturesque in the highest degree, while conspicuous in each are the Roman Catholic Church steeples, surrounded with their educational and charitable institutions. A great number of city people resort to these villages during the summer, and altogether from what I saw of them they appear to be in a most prosperous condition. From information received I learned that the chief industries are the wood-mill manufactories and the lumber exportation trade. The trees are sledged down in the winter, and shipped in spring to all parts of the world. To the scattered houses that connect the villages patches of agricultural land are attached, and the woods extending to far inland are used for grazing purposes. On the north side the valley opens out as we proceed upward, and the hills recede further and further into the background. The cultivated land here is subdivided up into the small sections characteristic of French farming, the result of continual subdivision of bequeathed properties. But you ask do all these rural families maintain themselves on these small patches of land ? The answer, as far as I could find out, is no, for, when not engaged

in cultivating the soil, many of the men are
employed in the lumber mills at home or in the
brick factories in the States and elsewhere, while
both the women and the children, when not
engaged in cod-fishing for the markets, weave
their own wool and make their own clothing.
Thus they manage to live in tolerable comfort and
to enjoy certain luxuries, while not a few have
considerable fortunes. The people are mostly all
French or of French descent, speak that language,
and manage their affairs according to French
law. The villages increase in size and importance
towards Montreal, at which the steamer arrived
after a twelve hours' run from Quebec.

## Montreal.

In approaching this splendid town one is at once
struck with the commercial enterprise and importance of the first city of the Dominion. The long
wharves, stretching for miles, are so crowded, and
the rivers so busy with crafts and steamers of all
sizes and of all nationalities, running in every
direction, that landing without collision or accident
requires the most careful and skilful handling. It
is almost incredible that the small Indian village
of Hochelaga when visited by Jacques Cartier in
1535 could develop into the imposing Montreal of
to-day with its 250,000 inhabitants. It is situated
on an island formed by the St Lawrence and
Ottawa rivers, with a history which is eventful
and interesting. The following description of
Hochelaga is from the pen of Cartier himself :—

"It is placed near, and, as it were, joined to a
great mountain, very fertile on the top, from
which you may see very far. The town is round,
encompassed about with timber, with three
rampires, one within another, framed like a sharp
spire, but laid across above. The middlemost of
these is made and built in a direct line, but perpendicular. The rampires are framed and fashioned
with pieces of timber laid along the ground, very
well and cunningly joined after their fashion ; this
enclosure is in height about two yards ; it hath
but one gate or entry thereat, which is shut with
piles, stakes, and bars ; over it, and also in many
parts of the wall, there be places to run along, and
ladders to get up, all full of stones, for the defence
of it. There are in the town about fifty houses,

each 50 paces long, and 15 or 20 broad, built all of wood, covered over with the bark of the wood, as broad as any board, and cunningly joined together. Within are many rooms, lodgings, and chambers. In the midst of every one there is a great court, in the middle whereof they make their fires. They live in common together, then do the husbands, wives, and children, each one, retire to their chambers. They have, also, in the tops of their houses certain garrets, wherein they keep their corn to make their bread. The people are given to no other exercise, but only to husbandry and fishing for their existence."

Having satisfied himself as to the nature and extent of the village, Cartier was conducted by a native escort to the top of the mountain, and from its summit he descried an immense extent of lovely country, interspersed with islands, hills, woods, and rivers, which filled him with feelings of pleasure and joy. In loyalty to his sovereign, he named the elevation on which he stood Mount Réal—Mount Royal—which name has since been extended to the city.

Cartier was evidently well received by the natives, who, in exchange for knives, beads, and other small trinkets, supplied him freely with fish and maize. Even in those early days Hochelaga claimed some importance, but nothing special has been mentioned in connection with it till 1611, when a trading post was established there by Champlain. Buildings were then erected, and, in order to test the fertility of the soil, some of the ground was cleared and seeds sown. Champlain held conferences with many of the Indian tribes who had come to interview him near the Lachine Rapids, and thereafter he returned to Quebec. Again, after a lapse of two years, he revisited Hochelaga, and penetrated farther into the country. No permanent establishment, however, was attempted on the island of Montreal till 1640, when a Society of thirty wealthy individuals was formed in Paris for the purpose of building fortifications to protect the colony against the Indian ravages, and for promoting religion therein. The King of France approved of the scheme, and Maisonneuve, a soldier of distinguished piety, knightly bearing, brave as a lion, and devout as a monk, was chosen as leader of the expedition. There was also secured to accompany him the services of a pious and virtuous woman, Jeanne Mance, to take charge of the sick and superintend the distribution of supplies. She was encouraged in the enterprise by the Queen of Austria and other distinguished ladies ; and one of these noble ladies provided her with means sufficient for the erection of an hospital. The expedition being ready, two vessels sailed from the fair coast of France, one bearing the leader, a priest, and twenty-five men, the other Mademoiselle Mance, a missionary, and twelve men, so that with the opening of the navigation of the St Lawrence in 1642 they took possession of Montreal on the 18th day of May by the celebration of solemn mass.

During the first few years the colony was constantly harassed by the Indians, and managed only to subsist with difficulty. The colonists were reinforced by one hundred soldiers from France in 1652, but this did not bring peace and prosperity to the colony; and the most sanguinary cold-blooded skirmishes were constantly engaged in till about 1700, when a great peace was concluded between the Iroquois on the one hand and the Hurons, Ottawas, &c., on the other. But notwithstanding this treaty, fortifications continued to be erected about the town, and whatever protection they might afford against the Indians, they were ill-calculated to withstand artillery, as was proved some fifty years later.

After the capture of Quebec in 1760 attention was directed to Montreal as the last stronghold occupied by the French in America. Hence it became indissolubly connected with the thrilling events of the conquest. The British plan of campaign was to hem Montreal in on all sides. How this had been successfully carried out, and how, after Levis had fired his last musket and Vandruil had exhausted all his powers of deplomacy, there followed a capitulation which transferred to Great Britain the fairest colony of France, are facts too well known to be enlarged upon here. It is unfortunate that the exact spot where the articles of surrender were signed has never been definitely ascertained, and that more than one place is left to claim this honour or disgrace.

At this time Montreal was a fairly large and important town, protected by rampart, ditch, and citadel—the batteries of the latter commanding the streets from one end to the other. It contained many first-rate churches, convents, and other public buildings, the most substantial being the officers' quarters and the palace of the Governor.

The St Lawrence about 1805 was not navigable as far up as Montreal by vessels carrying more than three hundred tons, so that its foreign trade was conducted by small barges and crafts, but now ocean steamers of 5000 tons charge and discharge cargoes on the wharves. The turning point in the mercantile history of the city happened about 1850, when the now floating palaces of the Allan Line and other steamship companies began to make their appearance in the St Lawrence. Then followed the construction of the Lachine and other canals; while the introduction of the Grand Trunk Railway had a powerful effect in making the city what it truly is—a busy, healthy, prosperous, and flourishing commercial centre, and destined for even greater things in the near future. Its importance may be gathered from the fact that no less than ten steamship companies are engaged in carrying on its trade by sea; and the inland traffic conducted by canals, rivers, and lakes, is immense; while it is the centre of seven railway lines, chiefly controlled by the Grand Trunk and Canadian Pacific Railway Companies. Vast grain elevators, manufacturing establishments, and the far-reaching grain, cattle, and provision trade of the great west and north-west, bid fair to make Montreal the rival of New York. Practically, the city is divided into two parts, and inhabited by two nationalities, which live entirely apart, unless in a few isolated cases, the English and the French. The western part of the city is altogether English-speaking, and the majority of them are Scotch. In none of the colonies, however, have both English and Scotch men made more of their opportunities than in Montreal. The eastern portion is purely French. They are a hard-working, thrifty, and honest race. The old people do not speak English, but the rising generation speak both languages equally well. Among them is a great deal of hoarded wealth, but, unlike most people, they are extremely particular how they invest their money. Although very hospitable and fond of society, it is difficult to gain access into the inner French circles; but once admitted there is found an amount of culture, grace, and refinement that surprises one. The conversational gift is almost universal, the newest topics of literature and art are discussed, and the ladies are familiar with all the political questions of the day. Just as the east and the west—the French and the English are exclusive of each other, so the south or Irish quarter is exclusive of both. It is known as Griffintown, and comprises a little world of its own, with shops, factories, schools, churches, &c. The Irish take a high position in business, politics, and society. Altogether, the inhabitants of Montreal are highly cultured, while the rising young men possess a dash of manly independence that promises well for future usefulness.

Montreal has two hundred miles of streets and lanes, grand specimens of architecture, wealthy banks, substantial public buildings, hospitals, charitable institutions, splendidly-equipped universities, colleges and schools, fine club houses, palatial private residences, public squares, parks, recreation grounds, and beautiful churches. Among the churches is the famous Notre Dame, second in America only to the Cathedral at Mexico, and intended to be a representative of the Notre Dame in Paris. Its tower is 227 feet high, and contains a peal of eleven bells. The "Gros Bourdon" in the western tower is reckoned among the five heaviest bells in the world. It weighs 24,780 pounds, is 6 feet high, and 8 feet 7 inches in diameter at the mouth. The nave of the church, including the sanctuary, is 220 feet long, 80 feet high, and 69 feet wide, exclusive of the side aisles, which measure $25\frac{1}{2}$ feet each, while the walls are five feet thick. The building will accommodate from 12 to 15,000 persons. It stands conspicuous, and in the tourist's mind forms a most notable landmark. The most historical and interesting square is that of Champ de Mars, which was a famous scene of promenade in the old French days, and, with the exception of the Plains of Abraham, there is no other piece of ground in America which has been so successively trodden by the armies of so many different nationalities in martial array.

Montreal is specially advanced in out-door sports, rod, gun, bicycle, football, golf, and lacrosse—the national game. During the winter skating is the most popular amusement, and the gaieties of the season are only surpassed by those of St Petersburg. It is extremely favoured with fine summer resorts and beautiful drives in the neighbourhood—the most delightful drive being to Mount Royal through the Mountain Park. A winding road of easy ascent leads up the mountain, with a ceaseless stream of carriages and pedestrians, to the summit, from which a view enchanting in beauty and variety is obtained. On a clear day the view is magnificent, several hundred feet below is spread out a gorgeous panorama of ever-varying beauty, and affording splendid and attractive views of the Canadian Metropolis and the noble river of the north, with its ceaseless traffic, the Victoria Bridge, and the foam of the Lachine Rapids. The broad landscape is dotted with comfortable homesteads, well-stocked and highly-cultivated farms, broad belts of forest extending here and there, and looming up like a mighty shadow in the distance, the far-off hills o Vermont tower their head, while winding through the valley the majestic St Lawrence rolls onward to the ocean. Handsome private dwellings, with beautifully laid out grounds, all contribute to the beauty and variety of a scene never to be forgotten.

It may be interesting to state that the St Lawrence river is 1500 miles long, and drains an area of 330,000 square miles. Between Montreal and Quebec it varies from one to two miles in breadth, while a short distance below Quebec it varies from ten to thirty-five miles in width. The tide rises fourteen feet at Quebec, but it ceases to be appreciable at the lower end of Lake St Peter. Among the few ports in America which the Great Eastern was able to visit on account of its great draught is that of Quebec, and between here and Montreal the depth is nowhere less than thirty feet. The distance from Montreal to the Atlantic Ocean is nearly 1000 miles. The city is 250 miles above salt water, and it is 315 miles nearer to Liverpool than the town of New York. The river water is utilised for all city purposes.

All the St Lawrence rapids are within easy reach of Montreal, but especially the famous Lachine Rapids, which should by no means be missed. Though this is the last in the chain of rapids, it is the most formidable and difficult to navigate. Flanked by the rocks on either side the steamer after the first pitch rises on the foaming billows, steered by the steady arm and sure eye of the man at the wheel. The peculiar feeling that comes over the passenger, and the roar of the water, command silence till the rapids ars run and the steamer emerges into the quiet current below. Then, taking a slight turn, the visitor gets a fine view of the Victoria Bridge— one of the wonders of the age—constructed by the Grand Trunk Railway Company to meet the requirements of their extensive traffic. The foundation stone was laid on 25th July, 1854, and the first passenger train ran across on 19th December, 1859. It is said to be about two miles long, and the cost of erection to have been close upon six and a-half million dollars. A little above is the beautiful steel bridge erected within more recent years by the Canadian Pacific Railway Company. The scene from the steamer deck is very grand, and commands a splendid panorama of the town and neighbourhood.

The Thousand Islands tour should be arranged at Montreal. These islands extend from Prescott to near Kingston, a distance of some fifty miles. This is the largest collection of river islands in the world, of every conceivable shape, appearance, and size, from a square foot to acres in extent. The largest are closely wooded, and the foliage is rich and lovely. On many of these islands are erected handsome hotels and the grand summer residences of the mighty dollar-making Americans. The steamer is frequently within a stonethrow from the shore of one of these, and now and again it looks as if further progress was impossible, when suddenly rounding a point channels and bays gradually open in front, and the visitor is whirled into a splendid amphitheatre of, to all appearance, a great lake, bounded on every side by an immense green bank, which, when approached, transforms itself into a hundred little island. Approaching the Thousand Islands Park, the most popular resort on the river, a beautiful view is obtained of crystal water studded by green islands, which stretch away and succeed each other as far as the eye can reach. This park began as a religious encampment under the Methodist organisation. Here several hotels and nearly four hundred cottages have been erected ; also, a large tabernacle for worship on the Sundays, and for lectures, concerts, and classes on week-days. The snowy tents of camping and picnicing parties are numerous. Yachting, boating, and fishing form the chief sources of amusement. These islands are also famous for wild fowl, which attract sportsmen from all quarters.

The distance from Montreal to Ottawa is traversed by rail in about four hours. During the journey many flourishing and prosperous villages are passed. Here and there are tracts of the original forests and well-cultivated fields, and, immediately on crossing a river, the fair capital of the Dominion is reached.

## Ottawa.

is a city with 50,000 inhabitants, surrounded by the grandest mountain, valley, river, and forest scenery. On a bold hill stand proudly and majestically the Parliament House of the Dominion and Government Buildings, all after the Gothic style of architecture, with towers, turrets, finials, and spires, forming a magnificent group. Of them a recent writer says—"Their splendour, their fine, commanding site, together with the beauty of the surrounding scenery, place them in a very enviable position compared with other structures used for similar purposes, and must ever be objects of interest to the tourist and stranger, and pride to the people of Canada." In the rear of these buildings stands the Library, octagonal in shape, dome-roofed, and with massive buttresses and finials. The inside of the building forms a great circular hall, in the centre of which there is a beautifully-executed life-sized marble statue of the Queen. The books are arranged in shelves round the circular wall, and number over 155,000 volumes. And there is every convenience, in the shape of seats, tables, &c, for the comfort and use of the numerous readers. To see this building and its contents alone is said to be worthy of a trip across the Atlantic.

The ground on which the city is built slopes gently towards the Ottawa river, and on the opposite bank of the river stands the little town of Hull, which is practically a suburb of the capital.

The imperial city is well laid out in fine broad streets, lined for most with beautiful trees, which in summer afford a grateful shade. Towards the outskirts, as in other towns, there are numerous suburban villas and the private residences of the wealthy citizens. They are beautiful in finish and architecture, and afford a proof of the taste and culture of the owners. In this town such facilities are given for building purposes that even clerks and tradesmen are able to erect comfortable and commodious self-contained houses for themselves. Living thus in houses apart, they enjoy higher privileges in the shape of privacy, &c., and greater immunities from all contagions, whether moral or physical, than those who are crowded together in the tenements which distinguish the like houses of our large towns. The public buildings are substantial and beautiful blocks of various styles of architecture. There are banks, hospitals, churches, monastic institutions, city halls, Post-Office, &c. The University of Ottawa ranks among the foremost in the Dominion, while the other educational institutions and schools are equipped by the leading scholars of the day. The hotels are large and comfortable, notably the Grand Union, Windsor, and Russel, the last mentioned having accommodation for five hundred guests. There are also some excellent clubs with large membership, and, without exception, all distinguished for their hospitality towards strangers.

The lumber mills are the largest and most perfectly equipped in the world, and a visit to them will prove most interesting and instructive. A visit to the factories, such as the paper-making, match-making, &c., will abundantly repay the visitor for his trouble for the knowledge they can so well afford to those interested in these several industries. The water and drainage system of the town are of the most complete description. Electricity plays an important part in the life of the capital. It is lighted by it; it affords the locomotive power of the street cars that continuously ply in every direction.

There are beautiful walks in and around the capital. A stroll along "Lovers' Walk" and through "Major Hill Park" is most enjoyable; and one may extend the pleasure by continuing the walk to Rockliffe Park, Rideau, and Chaudiere

Falls, which are but a short distance outside the city. Near Rideau Fall is Rideau Hall, the residence of the Governor-General, a fact which ought to make it interesting to English visitors. Considering its Imperial interests, the building seems small and insignificant, but here, notwithstanding, is the centre, not only of Canadian power, but also of the gaiety of its fashionable society life. It is surrounded by some eighty acres of land, finely laid out in parks, intersected by beautiful and shady drives. About two miles outside the city is the

## Experimenta lFarm.

Eight or ten years ago the Government considered the advantages that would likely accrue to the farming industry of the Dominion by the establishment of experimental farms. Accordingly, a select Committee was appointed, with the result that at present five of these are established in the most suitable centres in Canada, viz., one in Nova Scotia, one in Manitoba, one in North West Territory, one in British Columbia, and this one in Ottawa, which is the central one. For it five hundred acres were purchased by the Government in the near vicinity of the capital. The land, though somewhat swampy and not broken up at the time it was purchased, yet afforded many advantages for the purposes for which it was selected on account of the nature and quality of the soil. What was then practically a wilderness has been transformed into a series of well-appointed fields and testing plots, with commodious and suitable dwellings for the superintendents of the different departments, and model steadings. In the working of the farm are introduced all new implements, new machines, new manures, new seeds, and all the new methods that are likely to produce good results in developing a higher state of farming. Numerous and various experiments are constantly being made to test the earliness of the many varieties of cereals, their respective superiority in yield, stiffness of straw, quality of grain, so also they are continually experimenting how to produce the best root crops, the best grass and fodder crops, &c. There is a good chemical laboratory, fitted with the best appliances for the analysis of soils, fodder, plants, grasses, sugar, beet, &c.

The Entomologist is engaged in the subjects of insects injurious to crops and the remedies for their destruction. The horticulturist has made a vast collection of fruit trees and small fruits, together with a numerous assortment of vegetables, which have all been tested as to earliness, quality, &c. The diseases which affect fruit trees and vines are carefully observed, and remedies tried and recommended. The poultry manager is ready to give advice as to the management of fowls and the selection of the best variety of breed to adopt. The agriculturist has charge of the stock, and has introduced many new and important modes of feeding. It was he who designed the dairy building and piggery, which are on the newest principles, and form a good model for all buildings of a like kind. Valuable experiments are carried on in connection with the feeding of cattle and swine, &c., but probably the most interesting experiments are to be seen in the manufacture of butter. The visitor may see the qualities of the milk tested and converted into butter directly it is taken from the cow. The results of the experiments are published, and communicated to the senders free of charge. And there is reason to believe that samples from this country would be welcomed and treated in the same way as those received within the Dominion. Could not some of our home farmers try the experiment by sending samples or otherwise? Altogether a more profitable and instructive day than that spent on the farm at Ottawa cannot be conceived by those interested. Let it be added that the managers of the different departments are anxious to communicate all the knowledge they acquire, and to show the visitor everything. The civil, courteous, and obliging manner in which they do so is no small inducement to the tourist to repeat the visit, and at least his visit is certain to give him much new information worth digesting.

The sportsman and the naturalist will find the capital a centre of unrivalled attractions. Fish of all kinds, from five to fifty pounds, abound in the rivers and lakes, flocks of wild duck in the swamps, and partridge on the moor, with numerous deer in the woods, are surely sufficient inducements to visit what has been justly styled the "Sportsman's Paradise."

Ottawa received its name from the river on

whose banks it stands, and is intersected by the Rideau Canal, with the construction of which in 1826 it originated. The natural advantages of its location at the confluence of the Ottawa with the Rideau and Gatineau rivers are unrivalled, and to this the wonderful progress it has made is due. All three rivers drain an enormous district, rich in agriculture and timber. The timber is conveyed from the upper regions in enormous rafts to this point, but it is impossible to convey them unbroken over the Chaudiere Falls. Here, therefore, they are arranged and carried over in timber slides to the navigable water below without suffering any damage. And one of the most novel and exciting feats undertaken by almost all tourists, from the Prince of Wales downwards, is to descend these slides on a crib of timber. The importance of the position of what was originally a shanty village may be gathered from the fact that by 1854 the population amounted to 10,000, and that the honours of a city were conferred upon it in the following year. It was then divided into five wards, each being represented in the Council by three Aldermen. The new city grew rapidly, and, with the completion of the Government Buildings in 1865, a large influx of public officials came in. Within the last ten years it has doubled, not only in population, but also in commercial enterprise and wealth.

There is no city in Canada easier of access or affording better and quicker facilities for reaching all parts by rail and boat. In this fact, as well as in its being the outlet of the vast and varied resources in the regions beyond, the future greatness and prosperity of the fair capital of the Dominion chiefly lie. The inexhaustible lumber of the inland districts, the mineral wealth of the vicinity, which include gold, silver, copper, iron, lead, marble, and, in short, all minerals except coal, assure it of unlimited prosperity and expansion. But for this only want of coal, meantime, mining operations of all descriptions would have been extensively and successfully carried on. There are also the agricultural resources. As yet the fringe of all these is barely touched, and, when they are fully developed, who can estimate the commercial importance, the wealth, the greatness in the near future of this queen of cities?

It is with considerable reluctance that we leave the fair capital on the hill and set forward to Toronto, a city distant s me 230 miles. During the journey many important villages and a few towns are passed, all evidently in a thriving and prosperous condition, and engaged mostly in wood manufacture or in mills of various descriptions. After passing Perth the country is more or less covered with forests and partly broken. The next largest centre is Peterboro' with 10,000 inhabitants. Here the water power is immense, and utilised by many great manufactories and mills. Then follow a close succession of stations built chiefly for the convenience of the agricultural interests of the country, which is rich in oats, rye, wheat, barley, butter, cheese, and fruit, while cattle rearing is prosecuted with success. After a seven hours' run on the rail from Ottawa the train arrives at

## Toronto.

This is the capital of Ontario, and probably the most prosperous and progressive city in Canada. For the earliest mention of it we are indebted to the French memoirs of 1686, where reference is made to the "Portage of Toronto." The name was originally applied to the whole district. The Indian name signifies "well peopled" or "place of meeting." The portage to the "place of meeting" started on the shores of the lake and penetrated far into the country. A fort was erected by the French near the Exhibition Buildings, of which the remains may still be seen. It was then known as Fort Rouillé, but latterly it was changed to Fort Toronto, and gradually the general name of the district became limited to Toronto—the then straggling brick village that extended along the bay of Lake Ontario.

Niagara was the seat of the Provincial Government till 1793, when it was transferred to Toronto, which name was changed to " York" in honour of Frederick, Duke of York, the son of the reigning monarch of the day—George III. However good the intention, the new name never appeared to have rolled so smoothly on the native tongue or to have become congenial to the soil. The original designation of the place has been preserved by

Tom Moore in his famous Canadian boat song, written in 1801—

I dreamt not then that ere the rolling year
Had filled its circle, I should wander here
In musing awe; should tread this wondrous world.
See all its store of inland waters hurled
In one vast volume down Niagara's steep,
Or calm behold them, in transparent sleep,
Where the blue hills of old Toronto shed
Their evening shadows o'er Ontario's bed.

It had attained to such importance by 1834 that the honours of a city were conferred upon it, while the original designation of Toronto was substituted for "York," and enthusiastically received. Thus the shantie village grew with a comparatively uninteresting history until it was sacked and partially destroyed by the American forces in 1813. Time, however, has obliterated the old scars, and to-day there are no signs of the bloody frays and feuds of the beginning of the century. In 1879 the little "place of meeting" had a population of 71,000, while in 1892 it rose to 210,000, with 50,000 public buildings, a rate of progress of which the community have every reason to be proud. It is difficult to believe that so short a time ago the summer connection of Toronto with the outer world was only by water, and that in winter it was locked out from all communication except by sleigh. Yet so it was, and some of the older people remember the wonder with which the first locomotives were witnessed. It is now more than ever a favourite "place of meeting." And as in the days of yore the Indian tribes assembled here headed by their chiefs and patriarchs, so now there gather the social, benevolent, and commercial organisations from all parts of the Continent.

The people of Toronto are proverbially a Sabbath-loving and a Church-going community. No street cars are run, and hardly a wheel of any description turns on the Sabbath day. No shops are open, and no business of any kind transacted. It is pre-eminently a city of churches, there being close upon 200 churches and chapels. Their numerous spires and pinnacles rise conspicuously above the town. Many of them are unsurpassed in architectural beauty, symmetry, and design. There is St James' Cathedral—a fine specimen of Gothic architecture. Its gracefully-proportioned spire rises 316 feet, and is the highest on the

Continent. The tower contains a chime of bells
and a celebrated clock. The interior is beautiful,
and the stained glass chancel windows are after
the best art work of Munich. The tower and the
spire can be ascended, and a fine view is obtained
from the top of the city, the lake, and the country
around. There is the Metropolitan Church, the
headquarters of the Methodists of Canada,
magnificently situated in an open square. Its many
finials distinguish it from all other churches, while
its organ, with 3315 pipes, is the largest in
Canada.

But if Toronto is famous for its churches, it is
no less celebrated for its educational institutions.
There is a first-rate university, some seven colleges,
and nearly as many schools. They are all beautiful, massive and commodious buildings. The
higher branches are all taught successfully, while
at the head of the educational department is Dr
M'Lellan, a worthy and excellent Scotchman.
The public buildings are altogether creditable and
of a high order—notably, the Union Station, Post-
Office, Custom House, Banks, Theatres, Grand
Opera House, Hospitals, Reformatories, Halls,
and Picture Galleries. These latter should by
all means be visited. The paintings are splendidly
displayed, and represent all the European schools.

Toronto is divided into six wards, each ward
being represented in the city council by four
aldermen. It enjoys certain advantages over other
towns and municapilities arising from large tracts
of freehold property in the best business localities,
and from the lease-holders of these a large annual
revenue is derived. The streets are laid out at
right angles to each other, and, while this
faciliates the movements of the traffic, it does not
tend to improve the picturesqueness of the town.
The streets are all wide, with massive and substantial blocks on either side, many boulevarded
and block-paved, and most of them fringed with
trees, which contribute greatly to the appearance.
Yonge Street is perhaps the longest street in the
world. Its formation was contemplated in 1793
for a "portage to the upper lakes without the
necessity of going up Lake Erie and passing
Detroit." About forty years ago part of this
magnificent street was simply a slough of despond,
with water and mud that could scarcely be passed
over by the old ox carts. There flourished along

the once muddy part of this street a worthy tanner whose name is perpetuated by the "Bible House." The site on which it stands was bequeathed by him to the Bible and Tract Society on condition that the rent proceeds be expended in procuring Bibles to be annually distributed in the public schools. This annual ceremonial is discharged with great interest. Yonge Street was built and laid out as a Government undertaking for forty-six miles, and became the main artery extending north, and was lined with settlers' dwellings. Here is an incident worth noticing. "A story is told of a tourist newly arrived at York, Toronto, wishing to utilise a stroll before breakfast by making out as he went along the whereabouts of a gentleman to whom he had a letter. Passing down the hall of his hotel, he asked in a casual way of the book-keeper—"Can you tell me where Mr So-and-so lives?" (leisurely producing the note from his breast pocket); " it is somewhere along Yonge Street here in your town." "Oh, yes," was the reply, when the address had been glanced at, " Mr So-and-so lives on Yonge Street, about twenty-five miles up."

King Street, as the main street of the original village, is now the finest street in Toronto. The " Old Gaol" occupies the site on which once stood the Parliament Buildings of the Province of Upper Canada. They were wood erections of no great elegance, but sufficient for the accommodation of the Courts of Justice and the Legislature of that day. They were destroyed, with all the papers and records and a valuable library, during the American War, while the city itself was ransacked and pillaged. And, strange to relate, the destruction of the Government Buildings at Washington by the British forces a few months later was considered a just and sufficient reparation for the former havoc. On the other side of King Street, in front of St James' Cathedral, was the old market stance, where, curious enough, as late as 1834 the pillory and the stocks were set in order, and a woman condemned to undergo the ignominy of the pillory for two hours on two market days for being what was termed " a nuisance." These barbarous instruments of torture have been removed, and the fair ladies of Toronto are free from the fear of any such punishment, or even from any such unwarrantable imputations. A stroll along King Street during the fashionable afternoon hour will convince any stranger that, in appearance, comeliness, dress, and gaiety, the ladies of Toronto are second to none in the old country.

Toronto is beautifully situated on the shores of Lake Ontario, consequently the heat is tempered by a cool breeze from the water. Whatever may have been the heat during the day, it seldom continues into the night, and so, after the sun has set, the cool air and soft summer evenings make the town what it really is—a most enjoyable and pleasant summer resort.

## Toronto to Niagara Falls.

Starting by steamer from Toronto early in the morning the visitor may spend five hours at the Falls of Niagara and return in the evening. The trip is most delightful. Lake Ontario is 180 miles long, 234 feet above sea level, and 35 miles broad by the steamer route to Queenston. The distance is accomplished in about two hours by the beautiful and well-equipped steamers that have recently been placed at the disposal of the public. These have promenade decks, and are provided with seats and comfortable arm chairs for the pleasure of the passenger. On leaving the pier it seems almost impossible that the steamer should avoid coming into collision with some of the many pleasure boats plying by sail or oar in all directions, and presenting a most lively and exciting scene. As the steamer gets outside the greater part of the boats on the lake, a fine view of Toronto's prominent buildings and church spires is obtained. The part of the city extending along the water edge is seen to advantage. Away to the right the city is seen to merge away into pretty villas, becoming more apart as they extend from the town. There the Victoria Park commences, which, according to the account of a fellow-passenger, is not too well kept. Further down the bank rises precipitously, and the soil facing the lake appears white mixed with red clay. Here the continual beating of the water undermines the bank from time to time, and, the earth falling into the water, is being swept towards the harbour, consequently

it is found necessary to dredge it constantly.
When about half-way across the lake the land
entirely vanishes out of sight for a little. But, as
the steamer ploughs on her way, it soon reappears
in long stretches clothed with forests, and dotted
here and there with white villas and houses along
the water line. As the mouth of Niagara river is
approached, one is struck with its narrowness
and attracted by the ruined fort that stands on
each side. These fortifications recall earlier wars
and struggles, and the moss and grass-covered
battlements are left to show how much the gallant
deeds of yore are appreciated by the present generation. They were formidable enough in their
day, but, like most of their class, they would be
useless toys in the presence of modern artillery.
It may be interesting to note how often they
changed hands with the varying success of war.
The roar of artillery and rifle crack no longer dis-
turb the shore of the lake, while the high banks of
the historic river are no longer paraded by men of
war, but thronged with country peasants, tourists,
and pleasure-seekers. The banks are becoming
famous as summer resorts for the people of the
United States, as well as Canada, but especially
for the people of Toronto. As the main outlet for
transportation from east to west, the mouth of
Niagara played an important part. Indian
tribes for long disputed and fought with
each other for its possession. Later
on the French entered into league with some of
the northern tribes, who sent five hundred
warriors to help them to seize the entrance to the
river. Their march, however, was intercepted by
another two of the most powerful and warlike
Indian tribes, and they were compelled to make a
speedy retreat to their own country, while the
French, thoroughly beaten and crestfallen, retired
to Montreal. Three years after this the French
again mustered sufficient courage to renew the
attack, and, after a series of pitched battles,
dispossessed the Indians. No sooner, however, did
the main body of the French army retire from the
garrison of Fort-Niagara than the Indians, who
had patiently waited their opportunity, made a
terrible onset, and recovered possession. Only ten
whites escaped to tell the awful tale. Shortly
after this disastrous defeat the Indians entered
into a treaty with the French, which led to the

fort being enlarged by four bastions and a store-house. Meantime a duel between the British and the French for the possession of the whole continent was in progress. As the war went on an attack was made on the forts, and many armed boats covered the lake in front of the fort, while a strong force was despatched to hem it in by land. The garrison held out nobly, replying to the furious cannonade from the lake, and engaging in bloody skirmishes and desperate sallies by land, till all their officers were either killed or captured. Then an honourable capitulation was granted ! And, in acknowledgment of their gallant defence, those of the garrison who survived were permitted to march out with all the honours of war, and then lay down their blood-stained arms on the shore of the placid lake. So the French posses-sion passed away, and the neighbour-ing forts on learning the result were struck with terror and surrendered almost without a struggle. In 1763 the Treaty of Paris was concluded, by which the whole of Canada and all the French possessions east of the Mississippi river were ceded to the British Crown. The British maintained a military post at Niagara, unmolested by the Indian tribes in the neighbourhood. And, though the east bank was transferred to the United States by the treaty of 1793, a strong British garrison was always stationed at Fort Niagara.

A writer in 1791 thus describes his visit—"Opposite the fort of Niagara, on a large flat point on the Canadian side of the river, is a town lined out, and lots given gratis to such as will undertake to build on it agreeably to a plan laid down by Government, which, to me, seems to be a good one ; half an acre is allotted for the stance of each house and garden, and eight acres at a dis-tance for enclosures, besides a large commonty reserved for the use of the town. Several people have taken lots here already, and no doubt, as the country advances in population, so will the town in building. In the event of the fort on the opposite (American) side being given up, it is said there is one to be erected on this side, and the ground is already marked out for this purpose."

The town mentioned here was Newark, after-wards changed to Niagara. The fort was Fort-George, constructed in 1792 with the view of commanding Fort Niagara, together with the anchorage and harbour within the mouth of the river. Subsequently Fort Missaaga was erected to command the Canadian side. The disturbances threatened by the Indians in 1792 were so alarming that a Council was summoned to meet at Fort Niagara, to which their chiefs, the Canadian and the United States Commissioners, were invited. During the conference the birthday of King George of England was celebrated, and the representatives were rather amused to find themselves celebrating a royal gala day.

The first Parliament of the province of Upper Canada is said to have been held within this fort in 1794, but before the close of the year the seat of Government was transferred to Toronto, which was then called "York." But in 1794 it was conceded, along with some other four forts, under Jay's Treaty. About twenty years after the Revolution the Union Jack was lowered from the ramparts of Fort Niagara as a last salute was fired. The garrison and guns were then transferred across the river to Fort George, so that Fort Niagara was handed over to the Americans, and the Stars and Stripes floated peacefully above its ramparts till 1812, when the war broke out again.

In 1812 Fort-George so effectually assailed its oponent on the other side of the river that the garrison was compelled to retire from it. An armistice, however, was entered upon by which they were permitted to re-occupy it, but, after a short interval, both forts again engaged in a destructive artillery duel which did not prove advantageous to either party, and resulted in equal damage to both forts. During the following spring, the Americans having collected a large number of ships and boats together, with a strong body of soldiers and seamen, embarked, and, under cover of a dense fog, forced a landing after a gallant struggle. The landing parties were protected by the high precipitous banks, while the ships firing over their heads shot down the Canadians on the level plain. The British at last, seeing that the American victory was about complete, spiked the guns, blew up the magazines, and retired with their shattered ranks to St David. Thus Fort-George was taken and occupied by the Americans, but during their possession many bloody skirmishes were engaged in. Finally the British managed to cut off their supplies and to hem them in on all sides, and so compelled the Americans to evacuate the fort. Before doing so, however, they set all the houses in Newark on fire, and by this cruel deed rendered the inhabitants houseless and homeless, and exposed to all the hardships of a severe and frosty winter. But, while this work of burning was going on, the sudden and unexpected advance of Murray's troops alarmed them to such an extent that they retreated, leaving the fort intact and 1500 tents standing on the field. Murray's followers determined to avenge the atrocious burning, and, accordingly, 550 gallant men, under cover of night, crossed the river, advanced stealthily at dawn with fixed bayonets, fell upon the pickets, killed them to a man, then rushed forward, and, by scaling ladders, gained the interior, and after a deadly conflict Fort-Niagara was again in British possession. The Union Jack floated proudly above the ramparts on both sides of the river; while the stars and stripes were sent as a trophy to the Governor-General, then residing in Montreal. A most desirous peace was concluded in 1815, and once more Fort-Niagara was gracefully given up, and the stars and stripes replaced the British flag. The natural advantage of both forts is recognised at once. At a point where the river merges into the lake the banks are pretty high on each side, the water deep, and the river narrow. The fortifications have been in the possession of three nationalities—French, British, and United States. The forts were twice stormed by the British, and from each of the others were they wrested at the point of the bayonet, and each time they retired in honour, and ceded them as a testimony of national goodwill. Better days have come, and the dismantled, moss-covered ruins are now all that remain of the stirring past—the shores of the lake and the banks of the river are no longer stained with blood ; while the guardians of both, instead of slaughtering each other, are now only rivals in prosecuting the arts of peace and goodwill.

But the steamer has not lingered with us all this time at the forts. She has entered the river, the narrowness of which impresses the stranger very much, and, heedless of the strong current, she pursues her course to Lewiston, a flourishing village much frequented by pleasure-seekers. Thence to Queenston, a beautiful and deservedly popular summer resort. The pier is crowded, and presents a lively and gay appearance. The tourists arriving and departing by the steamer are very numerous, and the greater part of them are from Toronto. Close to the landing is the terminus of the electric railway, which runs to Chippawa, a distance of twelve miles. The electric car route is certainly the best to go by to obtain a sight of every point of interest on the river to and beyond the falls. They are specially designed as observation cars, with seats fixed longitudinally, the one above the other, facing the river, so that passengers can view the scenery without rising from their seats. Private cars can also be provided on application being made in advance. But before going "on board," as the American says, we have a short time to linger about Queenston. It is a charming village, and historically interesting. Here the first Parliament of Canada met in primitive simplicity under the shade of a spreading oak. Here were the headquarters of the garrison. Here were stirring scenes, and here too was the theatre of deeds of valour. That this was so is at once impressed upon one by the massive and colossal monument that crowns the hill close by. Among the many battles fought in 1812 was that of

## "Queenston Heights."

The Americans, to the number of 5300, assembled at Lewiston for the purpose of attacking Queenston, which had only 1500 men. Under cover of a strong battery mounted on a high bank and commanding the opposite shore, thirteen boats boldly crossed the rapid river. They were opposed by a less formidable battery on Queenston Heights. Three boats put back, but ten landed and returned for a second load of troops. The Americans were getting the worst of the sharp firing that was, meanwhile, being carried on between both batteries, but an unexpected turn took place during the battle. A strong detachment of Americans rounded a point of the river unperceived, and ascended the rocks by a path considered impassable. They gained the crest of the hill, and, after a severe fight, the Canadians were obliged to retire to the village, leaving the battery to the enemy.

The cannonading carried on during the morning reached the ears of Sir John Brock, who was
stationed in Niagara. He thought the attack at
Queenston was only a ruse to draw the garrison
out of Fort-George, which he understood was then
to be attacked by the Americans, who were con-
cealed in boats behind a point near Fort-Niagara.
Before removing any of his troops, therefore, he
resolved to ride out and see for himself how
matters stood. Reaching Queenston with only
two *aides-de-camp*, he discovered the Americans,
by this time reinforced, in possession of the
heights. Orders were at once given for securing
more troops, and bombarding Fort-Niagara, which
latter was done with such effect that the
garrison had to evacuate the fort. General
Brock meantime resolved to retake the heights,
and, dismounting from his steed, charged on foot
at the head of 300 men. It was a desperate and
and bold attack made against a far outnumbering foe,
but it resulted in the Americans being beaten back
on to the slope of the hill. In the ascent General
Brock fell mortally wounded near a thorn bush
which marks the spot. His fall was not made
known at the time. Colonel M'Donald, his *aid-
de-camp*, was next shot while gallantly charging up
the heights with the York Volunteers. The
battery was, however, retaken, and the Americans
driven off. Some of their officers were about to
surrender, and hoisted a handkerchief upon a
bayonet, but a gallant youth valiantly tore it off,
and, encouraging his men, again opened fire. The
Canadians, much inferior from the first in
numbers, and now reduced by one-third killed
and their leaders dead, retired to Queenston
carrying the body of General Brock along with
them. The Americans were now in absolute possession of the heights, and their comrades on the
opposite side of the river, though they saw all
that had taken place, did not venture across to
their assistance. The Canadians, meantime reinforced, were led by a circuitous route, and,
attacking the Americans in flank, gained possession
of the heights. Both sides were about equal in
numbers; they were also equal in courage and
bravery. With a ringing cheer the Canadians
advanced to the charge, and the Americans. after
a short resistance, fled down the hill towards the
landing place. Such of them as tried to escape

through the woods were driven back, others, finding all escape cut off, went down the cliffs clinging to the bushes, and some of these losing their hold were dashed to pieces on the rocks below. Those who endeavoured to swim across perished in the attempt. The victory was most decisive. A flag of truce was hoisted, and about 1000 men surrendering were made prisoners. This was the result of the impetuous and gallant dash, made by General Brock, which had frightened the Americans, and prevented reinforcements being sent across the river. It must be admitted that the victory was dearly bought by the brave and gallant General's death. His remains were buried two days after in Fort-George with all military honours ; and, "as a mark of respect due to a brave enemy," the garrison, which had meantime re-occupied Fort-Niagara, with much generosity fired minute guns during the funeral Such was the termination of a battle gallantly and bravely fought by both sides. An armistice was agreed to as a condition of which the Americans engaged to destroy all their boats. This armistice was prolonged indefinitely. Niagara was freed from the invaders' presence, and Brock rests in memory as " the saviour of his country."

### LINES ON THE DEATH OF BROCK.

As Fame alighted on the mountain's crest
She loudly blew her trumpet's blast ;
Ere she repeated Victory's notes she cast
A look around, and stopped : Of power bereft,
Her bosom heaved, her breath she drew with pain—
Her favourite *Brock* lay slaughtered on the plain !
Glory threw on his grave a laurel wreath,
And Fame proclaims, " A Hero sleeps beneath."
—*Bruyères.*

Such is the history of the hero commemorated by the massive monument on the top of the hill, crowned by a colossal statue of the General in military uniform, the left hand resting on his sword, the right extended holding a baton. It is 185 feet in height, adorned with numerous figures and scenes of the battle. Beneath the column the remains of the General and his *aides-de-camp* who fell with him lie in stone sarcophagi. The gate on the principal entrance to the beautiful and well-kept grounds that surround the monument is adorned with the arms of the Brock family. The care-taker for a small fee will conduct visitors by the spiral stair to the summit of the monument,

from which a view of unrivalled beauty and
extent is obtained. The province of Ontario is
seen to stretch in one immense plain, while the
blue waters of the lake form a distant sky line.
The magnificent Niagara emerges from its deep
ravine, and in long reaches of lovely green is seen
to slowly wind its way towards the lake. The
country all around has the appearance of land
comfortably settled, widely cultivated, and beautifully clothed with trees. The church spires of the
towns and villages near at hand are seen ; the
position of those further off is indicated by the
curls of smoke rising above them like gleaming
white dots. Altogether the scene is one of most
exquisite beauty, and it impresses one with the
fact that this whole country is one of boundless
wealth and exuberant fertility.

The monumental stone a little way down the
slope of the hill indicates the exact spot at which
the General received his death-wound. The first
monument, erected by the British Government in
1826, was destroyed by means of explosives, used
by a vandal who was afterwards imprisoned for
the dastardly deed. But the present one was
erected in 1853 by his grateful countrymen. Some
idea of the fervour which raised this splendid
monument some twenty-eight years after the
death of the hero may be gathered from one of the
speeches which were then delivered at a gathering
of 8000 people assembled from all parts of the
country. One of those who served under Brock
said—" Looking at the animated mass covering
these sacred heights in 1840, to do honour for a
war in 1812, now old in history, one is prompted
to ask, ' How comes it that the gallant General
has left so lasting an impression in the hearts of
his countrymen, how comes it that the fame of
Brock thus floats down the stream of time, broad,
deep and fresh as the waters of the famed river
with whose waves it might be almost said his life's
blood mingled ?' In reply, we might dwell on his
civil and military virtues, his patriotic self-devotion,
his chivalrous gallantry and his triumphal achieve-
ments. Still, there was more that gave him talismanic
influence and ascendancy over his fellow men, and
which he wielded for his country's good. His was
the mind instinctively to conceive and promptly
to dare—incredible things to feeble hearts. With
skill and bearing he infused his chivalrous and

enterprising spirit into all his followers, and impelled them to realise whatever he boldly led the way to accomplish."

We will now return to the steamer wharf, and "board" the electric car by which passengers are carried along the bank of the river. The grade up the hill is pretty steep to begin with, and the first stop is made at Queenston. Leaving the village, the road—or, as we would say, the railway line—passes near the monumental stone erected in 1860 by the Prince of Wales to mark the exact spot where General Brock fell. Then it passes over the famous battlefield, and close by the monument described above. The car is now very near the gorge, and commands a splendid view of the lower rapids all the way till the world-renowned whirlpool is reached. It is a huge basin, with banks rising perpendicularly to a height of 250 feet. The current whirls round and round this basin with great velocity. Crossing the viaduct over the whirlpool ravine is rather exciting, and the view below grand. But the tourist should descend by the inclined railway, as the view from below is much finer. Here the water seems to churn itself up into a boiling mass of foam. As we proceed the Railway Suspension Bridge and the Cantilever Bridge are passed. The new foot and carriage suspension bridge comes next, and in a couple of minutes after the car stops at Clifton House, the best Hotel on the Canadian side. Here the famous falls are seen, and their spray comes up in showers.

## Niagara Falls.

It would be vain to attempt to describe Niagara Falls. The greatest word-painters have failed to pourtray them ; poets have sung of them, but the grandest flights of imagination in poetry or prose convey but a very vague idea of the sublimity of the scene. The power and majesty of the Creator as exhibited in the stupendous cataract call forth the adoration of the creature—man. The overwhelming grandeur and majesty fill the mind of the spectator with awful veneration and profound solemnity as he thinks of Him who holds the water in the hollow of His hand. They change with every sunbeam, assume a new appearance, inspire fresh interest, and compel new admiration. At first sight many think the Falls disappointing.

They go there hardly knowing what to expect, and, when they see it, conclude the spectacle is not what it was represented to be. The scene at the Falls grows upon one, and the more the stranger gazes upon them the more profoundly he is impressed. No person can spend a few days about the Falls without in some measure appreciating their overwhelming grandeur and magnitude. Their roar is sometimes deafening, but that depends upon the wind and upon the state of the atmosphere. It is not unfrequently heard fifteen or twenty miles distant, but at other times it is scarcely noticed half-a-mile away. For a mile around every open door and window will sometimes tremble. The roar, on rare occasions, has even been heard at Toronto, a distance of forty-four miles. The visitor should not miss a trip on the Maid of the Mist, as the steamer which shoots the rapids is called. The sail is a little exciting as she nears the foot of the falling water and comes almost under the sheet. The spray sometimes dashes over, but the passenger is protected by the water-proof suit provided on board. But perhaps the most interesting feature is the beautiful rainbow colours that appear to stream in every direction upon the water and spray.

Donning a rubber suit on the Canadian side and descending by the "lift," then passing through the tunnel and right under the fall, forms a very interesting experience, and gives one a novel sensation. This little trip should be undertaken and repeated on the American side from Goat Island to the "Cave of the Winds," and out on the bridges and platforms. Here the falls are tumbling down at your feet, you are surrounded with heavy spray, and almost deafened with the roar and tumult. It is necessary to secure a guide, who provides the waterproof suit.

Some extraordinary feats have been performed in and about Niagara River and Falls. Captain Webb's fatal swim is one of the most recent. He was an Englishman by birth, and while yet a youth he ran away to sea and became famous for his swimming feats. His first laurels as a public swimmer were won in South Africa in 1872; and for saving the life of a sailor who was washed overboard he was presented with £100 by the passengers. On swimming across the Channel he was presented by the Prince of Wales with £5000.

After many such feats he took up his residence at Boston, where he left his wife and two children when he started for Niagara. Captain Webb publicly intimate 1 his intention to swim the rapids on 24th July, 1883, and many spectators gathered to witness the event. Leaving Clifton House on the date mentioned at four P.M., he proceeded down the bank to the ferry landing, where he stepped into a small boat rowed by the ferryman to near mid-river. There he jumped from the boat into the river, and swam leisurely down towards the rapids, keeping, to all appearance, perfect control over himself till he reached the height of the rapids opposite the whirlpool rapids elevators, and there, in the raging surge, he disappeared for ever. His body was found four days after floating on the water about a mile below Lewiston. Never was physical courage worse applied than in this brave fellow's last adventure. He was only thirty-five years old at his death. Even had he been successful, no practical service would have been rendered to the world by the feat. The Niagara River is the channel through which the vast surplus waters of Lakes Superior, Michigan, Huron, and Erie is passed into Lake Ontario, and thence by the river and gulf of St Lawrence into the ocean.

The cataract is formed by the descent of the Niagara River down a ledge of rocks, more than one hundred and sixty feet of perpendicular height, into a basin of unknown depth below. From Niagara Falls the tourists sometimes go on by Buffalo, but we returned by the same route to Toronto.

The distance between Toronto and Owen Sound is traversed by rail in about four hours. The villages and stations passed on the route appear to be flourishing and prosperous. They form farming centres, and afford substantial evidence of the fertility of the plateaus and valleys surrounding them. The country in a few places close to the railway line is not too rich, nor too closely wooded, though prosperous farmsteads and stretches of fertile land are numerous. At one junction an enormous elevator is seen, and on the route many sawmills are swept by. The streams and lakes in the district are numerous, and abound in fish, which—to judge from the flies that you see hooked round so many of the passengers' caps—

attract many anglers. From the appearance of
the rural people about the stations, the large
majority might be set down as Scotch and Irish.

## Owen Sound.

Arriving at Owen Sound, the station is crowded
with gay tourists, and the whole presents a lively
and pleasing appearance, which is enhanced by
the beautiful steamer at the wharf, about forty
yards from the train. Owen Sound has a population of over 8000. From its situation on the
Georgian Bay it is the central port for the steamer
sailings, and the shipping point of an immense
farming district, and, therefore, it is rapidly
growing in importance. The country about is
closely wooded, and the town itself is well
sheltered by a high amphitheatre of limestone
rock. It is visited during the summer by a large
number of tourists, who chiefly delight in the
shooting and fishing afforded them in the vicinity.
The various trades common to such towns are
vigorously pushed forward, especially the manufacture of furniture and woodware.

The Clyde-built steamer of the Canadian Pacific
Railway Company upon which it was our lot to
embark was the Manitoba, a magnificent steel
vessel of 2000 tons, elegantly appointed and
illuminated throughout with electric light. The
state-rooms, which are arranged side by side right
round the dining and drawing-room saloons, contain two berths and a lounge each. They are
roomy, well ventilated, and to them passengers
can retire for a comfortable lounge or a quiet read.
A walk round the fine promenade deck seven
times is calculated to be a mile ; and round it in
couples the passengers are continually tramping to
raise an appetite and keep the constitution in good
order. No intoxicating liquors are sold on board,
so that those who require stimulants must provide
themselves with them before embarking. On the
arrival of the train the steamer is prepared to
start whenever the passengers are all on board.
She then steams out of the Georgian Bay, passing
its bold woody headlands to Lake Huron, and then
into a fairy-land of narrows, islands, and forest-
clad hills. Here the steamer is sometimes within
stone-throw of land, and seems so hemmed in as if
further progress were impossible. But on she goes
guided by the steady arm at the wheel, and the

constant use of the steam whistle wakening the echoes around. Tugs and crafts of all sizes are passed in great numbers.

## Sault Ste Marie.

Arriving at Sault Ste Marie, the long rapid of the same name is seen from the deck of the steamer to great advantage. It stretches for about three-quarters of a mile in length, the water rushing down with great fury and breaking over the rocks in surging waves. This is the outlet from Lake Superior to Lake Huron, and an enormous quantity of water pours through it. It is interesting to watch the Indians poling their canoes up the surging rapids, and peering through the clear waters to see if any fish are swimming in the hollows among the rocks, then suddenly dropping down with the swift current they sweep them out with long-handled scoop nets. The passengers have time to enjoy an exciting run through the rapids in an Indian canoe, or to stroll through the town while the steamer is passing through the canal. She takes about an hour and a half to do this. The locks that have been constructed on the American side are magnificent. The canal on the Canadian side is only in process of construction. The importance of the locks may be estimated from the fact that a greater aggregate of tonnage passes through them during the navigation season than is shipped through the Suez Canal in a whole year. By means of the canal the vessel is raised some eighteen feet to the level of Lake Superior. Sault Ste Marie and the neighbouring villages are growing rapidly, and becoming popular summer resorts owing to the facilities of communication afforded by land and water. The three great railways that have converged in Sault Ste Marie within recent years have given the villages a great impetus. The Canadian Pacific Railway Company have spanned the rapids by a magnificent steel bridge. As a centre for excursions by land and lake, the town is most favourably situated ; the three great lakes of the new world meeting here. But while we were ashore the steamer has gained the top lock, and we must re-embark before she emerges into Lake Superior. It is 460 miles long, 170 miles broad, and 800 feet deep, being thus 200 feet below the level of the

Atlantic. Through the broadest part of this immense lake the steamer strikes a direct course till the rocky bluffs of Isle Royal come in sight. Then comes Thunder Cape, 1380 feet high—a bold purple promontory sloping gently for a short distance from the lake and then rising in a perpendicular cliff. It stands grandly at the entrance to a bay of the same name, which is partly formed and sheltered by it. Behind it is Silver Islet, from whose depths many millions in value of silver have been dug out, but the mines have become too difficult for profitable working, so that the miners are now continuing their operations upon the mainland. Thunder Bay, when fairly entered, is almost surrounded by a high mountain range mostly covered with wood. As the steamer strikes for Port Arthur the scenery is fine all round. This town boasts of 4000 inhabitants, and the passengers have an opportunity of seeing it while the vessel is discharging her cargo. The buildings are good, and there are some fine shops. Conspicuous among the latter are the jewellers, where brooches, rings, &c., mounted in the beautiful-coloured stone of the district, are much run upon.

Leaving Port Arthur, the steamer, after sailing for an hour along the shore, arrives at

## Fort William,

overshadowed by the Mackay Mountain, of which a good view is obtained from the deck of the ship. The population of the town is about 3000. That it is rapidly becoming a commercial centre of importance is evident from the piles of coal that are heaped on the wharf for transmission inland, the great elevators, three of which contain from twelve to fifteen hundred thousand bushels each, that stand close by, and the great activity all round. Its accessibility by land and water, combined with the beauty of its location, and the opportunities for sport in the vicinity, are making it a favourite resort for pleasure seekers. Fort William was at one time a Hudson's Bay Company's post, and did an extensive trade in fur. The journey from Owen Sound to this town occupies two days and two nights. And no one who has been favoured with good weather is ever likely to forget the impressions made by so fine a trip. The comfort of the steamer ploughing through the glassy lakes, that look more like oceans than lakes, the rapids, the narrows, the islands, that have been passed, and the land scenery, all combine to entrance the mind. Here our happy company, who had been having a most enjoyable time of it on board the steamer, break up with regret. Between the arrival of the steamer and the departure of the west-bound transcontinental train the traveller has sufficient time to have a good look at the town if he so desires.

## Fort William to Winnipeg.

The journey from Fort William to Winnipeg, occupying a night and the greater part of a day, is through a wild broken country, rocky, and for most clothed with immense forests. The rivers that pour down the mountain sides are rapid, and show the pressure of water from above. The many cataracts and waterfalls passed are most picturesque, as are also the numerous lakes along the line. The valuable forests that clothe the hills have been swept by fires, as is evidenced from the blackened stumps and naked, withered branches, with their ghost-like and weird appearance in the moonlight, standing out against the sky. This wild region was traversed by Wolseley for 400 miles, when he successfully led an army to suppress the rebellion of the half-breeds on Red River in 1870. A few of the boats used on the expedition may yet be seen from the railway. But, wild and broken as the country looks, it abounds in precious metals, valuable minerals, and other natural wealth, while it supplies the boundless prairies beyond with the much-needed timber. Right in the heart of this wilderness is the beautiful island-dotted Lake of the Woods. It is the largest sheet of water seen from the railway between Lake Superior and the Pacific Coast. Here one is surprised at the industry carried on. The convenient water power is utilised by quite a number of sawmills with their tall black chimney stalks. Quite a cluster of warehouses and elevators are overshadowed by an enormous flour mill with a grinding capacity of 2000 bushels per day. It is an imposing block of five or six stories high, and built of granite quarried on the spot. Large sawmills appear in close succession westward, while the stations are busy with the transportation of the immense piles of timber, sawn for all purposes, that are heaped up ready for shipment. The wood trade is mostly carried on by Eastern Canadians—a hardy race, born to the work—who prefer the ground thus cleared to the ready-made farms of the West. The villages increase in size and importance as the train gradually gets nearer the prairie, till, leaving the woods behind, the valley of the Red River is run up, and the river crossed by a long iron bridge. Here a blink of crafts and steamers is got, and then the famous city of Winnipeg comes into view, and is soon thereafter entered.

## Winnipeg.

It is scarcely credible that the frontier trading post, known a few years ago as Fort Garry, should have been transformed into a town of 30.000 inhabitants, but yet such is Winnipeg. While yet an important station of the Hudson's Bay Company, it came prominently into public notice during the Red River Rebellion of 1869, when Riel, the half-breed, led the Insurrectionists. But a great change has come over the city since that time : the canoes on the river have been replaced by powerful steamers, and the waggon cart supplanted by the iron horse. Fort Garry, the home of the Indians, was always an important trading centre, and early visited by the Hudson's Bay and North-West Companies. The former did an extensive trade with the Indians in the exchange of furs for merchandise ; and the business relationship that always existed between them and the wild tribes had a most healthy influence. Indeed, it is owing to their kind dealings with the Indians that is to be attributed the friendly manner in which the Indians received the British advances.

Winnipeg is the "golden gate" to the North-West, and the half-way house between Montreal and Vancouver. It is built at the juncture of two rivers—the Red and the Assiniboine. Thus its natural position will always keep it in the front rank of commercial enterprise. The enormous net-work of railways connecting it with all parts, surrounded by a fertile country, and in direct communication with the vast wealth extending between it and the Pacific coast, augur well for its future prosperity. Its rapid growth has also been thus graphically described—"It may be truly said that Manitoba is the beginning of a vast grassy sea of virgin wealth—of a boundless prairie of untold fertility, and at the outer rim of this wonderland sits, queen-like and majestic, young, but strong and lusty and prosperous—outstripping all its rivals, rapidly increasing in importance—an adolescent giant, whose yet untried strength is indicative of a sturdy manhood. In this place, midway between two great oceans, Winnipeg has sprung up as if by magic, as if in this latter day the genii of Aladdin's lamp had created a city in an incredibly short space of time. For sudden growth, combined with solidity, the world has probably never seen its counterpart. In a few years it has risen from a hamlet to a metropolis. There is no flimsiness about its buildings—no mere temporary makeshifts of structures, as in many of the mushroom towns which have risen on the western wilds. The first surprise excited in a stranger on visiting Winnipeg is its broad, paved streets, the substantiality and magnificence of the public buildings, the neatness and taste of the private residences, and the possession of all the accompaniments of metropolitan life. To-day it can, with pardonable pride, claim a development unparalleled in the history of Canada, and boast that its name, synonymous with all that is progressive and prosperous, is more widely and familiarly known in every quarter of the civilised globe than that of other cities of greater age and pretensions." It is remarkable that the resources of the North-West were so little known till within recent years. Now they are rapidly being taken advantage of in proportion to the access facilities afforded.

As the headquarters of the Winnipeg and Hudson's Bay Railway, a railway which is in the course of construction, it will be brought into closer connection with the mother country. Arriving at the station, the stranger is at once struck with its commodiousness, and the busy and active life of which it is the constant scene. It is provided with excellent waiting and refreshment rooms. The sidings of the train yard would extend, if stretched in a straight line, some twenty miles, while the engine sheds and workshops erected by the Canadian Pacific Railway Company would do credit to any country or town in existence. The land offices of the Company are within

the station buildings, and intending settlers bound
for the far west may there be conveniently supplied
with all information, and provided free with
innumerable pamphlets descriptive of the extent
and resources of the country. Adjoining the
station are the Government Land Offices, where
valuable information may be obtained on all
subjects.

The visitor will be agreeably surprised to see the
broad well-paved streets. The town is well
provided with handsome hospitals, splendid
schools, and beautiful churches. The buildings
generally are substantial and of a superior style of
architecture, as, for example, the Government,
municipal, and other public buildings, the hotels,
and the warehouses. Electric cars run in all
directions, and electric light is used all over the
town. The new streets that are being formed,
and the numerous new buildings in course of erection round all the outskirts of the city, are the
most convincing proofs of the demand for houses,
and, therefore, of the constant growth of the population. Among the most recent built stores are
those of the Hudson's Bay Company. This block
is entirely built of stone, and guaranteed fire-
proof. In these stores anything from "a needle to
an anchor" may be purchased at a reasonable
price. Since they carried on the seal and fur
trade with the Indians their methods of business
and the style of their buildings have
gradually changed to meet the modern
requirements of civilisation. A Hudson's
Bay Company store is to be found in
almost every important town, and the benefit it
confers on the community is incalculable. It
secures to them first-class goods at a moderate
price, and so prevents other tradesmen from
demanding exorbitant profits for goods supplied.
The settlers are therefore protected so far.

The only relic of the old Fort Garry which now
exists is the archway in front of the old Government House, but the foundations of the old stone
wall which surrounded it may be traced on close
inspection.

Winnipeg is the chief centre of the transcontinental railway system, and the headquarters
of the western division, which boasts of three
hundred elevators or grain stores, with warehouse
capacity for over seven million bushels. The

terminal elevators in the town have capacity for about half the quantity. There are important flour and oatmeal mills and large manufactories of various kinds. Owing to the unpopulated state of the prairie, it was only within very recent years that the latter industries were started. But now the unlimited water power, that can be easily utilised for the purpose, promises to make it a famous manufacturing centre. The quantity of oats, barley, wheat, and potatoes that are sold at Winnipeg is hardly calculable. But it is safe to say that in proportion to the population no town in the world transacts more business than this town.

About six miles from Winnipeg is Silver Heights, the property of Sir Donald A. Smith. Driving to it through the prairie, one is struck with the enormous cabbage, cauliflower, carrots, &c., that appear on either side. All sorts of garden produce grow here in the open fields, and their size is the best possible testimony to the climate and fertility of the soil. The last of the millions of buffalo that once roamed over the prairies are kept here in a protected park, and I had the pleasure of seeing some half-dozen of these noble animals.

Leaving Winnipeg, the capital of the Province of Manitoba, for the Far West, the tourist is first surprised to find so much of the prairie in the near vicinity of the town in its natural condition, unbroken, and sparsely inhabited. After the first surprise is over the locomotive pursues its course over a boundless level country extending as far as the eye can reach, and with nothing to break the view but a long line of trees that mark the course of the Assiniboine River. Herds of cattle, feeding on the rich green grass, appear on either side, and soon some splendid grain fields and homesteads at regular intervals are passed. The homesteads are surrounded with highly-cultivated land, and appear to be in a most prosperous condition. After a run of sixty miles from Winnipeg the train first stops at

## Portage=la=Prairie.

This is an important town of a day's growth, with over 4000 of a population. It is the centre of a rich district, as is evident from the flour mills and the large grain elevators that stand out conspicuously near to the station. From this town a branch line strikes off the main line in a north-westerly direction for some two hundred miles to Saltcoats, where so many families of the crofter class from the Hebrides acquired settlements a few years ago. Special facilities were afforded them by public subscriptions, augmented by the Imperial Parliament. They have no reason to regret their choice, and, from all information received, they appear to be quite content with their lot and doing well. The country, rendered accessible by this new railway branch, is extremely fertile, and intending settlers would do well to inspect it before proceeding farther west.

After leaving Portage-la-Prairie the country is well settled, and busy little towns with grain elevators are passed in pretty close succession till we arrive at

## Brandon.

This town has nearly 6000 inhabitants, is growing by leaps and bounds, and is second in importance only to Winnipeg. It is the distributing market centre of an extensive and well-cultivated district, as may be seen from the number of grain elevators, flour and saw mills. The town is beautifully situated on high ground, and, though only a few years old, can boast of splendid streets, beautiful buildings, and all the other institutions that are necessary to the development of a large, commercial, and prosperous city, such as it promises to be in the near future. The Experimental Farm is in the vicinity of Brandon. The success that attended many of the settlers in the neighbourhood of the town is almost incredible. Let me illustrate this by one example—Some eight or ten years ago a young man started life as a farm labourer ; his savings did not amount to much, but in a couple of years the modest sum at his disposal was laid out in securing for himself a half section, or 320 acres of land. Fortune smiled upon his efforts, and he went on adding more land to that originally acquired, till at the end of six years he had no less than 2000 acres under cultivation ; while the property increased in value to over £8000. Surely this instance should encourage farm labourers to go out and try their fortune. A branch line, from Brandon to the south-west, opens up a vast track of country,

rich in grain, and especially in coal, which is
being extensively worked and shipped. Another
branch line strikes off to the north-west, so that
both branches bring a large trade into the town.

## Over the Prairie.

After leaving Brandon, the train has fairly
reached the first of the great prairie *steppes* that
rise at long intervals towards the Rocky Mountains, and the undulating prairie is dotted over
with thriving villages and prosperous farms as
station after station is passed in close succession,
very similar to each other in everything but the
varying number of houses that have clustered
around them. The country traversed is covered
with short, thick, sweet grass, intermingled with
a great many flowers that give the landscape a
very pretty appearance. From among the grass
now and again may be seen flocks of "prairie
chickens," scared from their coverts by the passing train, rising on the wing. Wild geese and
duck are also abundant on the many ponds that
are seen from the train.

> In myriads o'er the prairie
>   Bright flowers bloom strangely fair ;
> There's beauty in the clear blue sky,
>   There's sweetness in the air ;
> And loveliness with lavish hand
>   Decks dell and dingle gay.
> Strange birds in painted plumage gay
>   In hundreds haunt the grove ;
> O'er marsh and moor the loon and heron,
>   The coot and plover rove.
>
> The clear Assiniboine winds free
>   Through many a fertile vale ;
> The antlered deer and graceful hind
>   Bound o'er the wooded dale.

There are thus excellent opportunities for sport.
The country hereabout is famous for the gigantic
potatoes produced, as well as for its enormous yield
of oats, rye, barley, and flax—in short, everything that grows in a temperate climate flourishes
here, and consequently it has become a very
favourite district for Britishers.

Indian Head may be said to be the centre of the
celebrated Bell Farm, which is 100 square miles
in extent. The furrows are said to be four miles
in length, and to plough one furrow outward and
another returning is half-a-day's work for a man
and a team. It is a veritable manufactory of

wheat, and the work is carried on son ewhat on a military style—"ploughing by brigades and reaping by divisions." The principal buildings of the farm may be seen from the train to the right, while the neat cottages of the workmen dot the plain as far as the eye can reach.

## Regina,

the capital of the Province of Assiniboia, some forty miles from Indian Head, is the next most important town, having a population of nearly 3000, being the distributing centre for the country north to Prince Albert and south to St Paul's. The Legislative Assembly of the North-West Territories meets here. About two miles beyond the station the Lieutenant-Governor's residence may be seen to the right, and on the same side, a little further on, are the head-quarters of the North-West Mounted Police. The officers' quarters, the barracks, and the drill hall form quite a little village by themselves. The organisation consists of 1000 young picked men, thoroughly drilled, and under the strictest military discipline. They hold a similar position to our policemen at home, and are stationed at intervals over the North-West Territories. Long before the introduction of the railway their conciliatory and affable manner commanded alike the respect, the confidence, and the submission of the Indians, so that the appearance of the red-coated guardians of the prairies was not attended by the violence and the bloodshed which characterised the opening of new districts in other parts of America.

The country, which surrounds Regina for about twenty miles, is known as the Regina Plain, and is supposed to be the best soil in Canada for growing wheat in a favourable season. I have been told by an eyewitness that a farmer sometimes takes four crops in succession off a field after the first ploughing, the stubble being simply burned, and the seed harrowed into the ashes. Think of that, almost a reversal of the curse! A number of families from Scotland have settled down in this district. They have had advanced to them, as an experiment, from £100 to £120 each. The money was chiefly laid out upon their homesteads, and the progress that is being made by them is watched with considerable interest.

From Regina a railway branch extends south

and north, the latter opening up the Saskatchewan
country as far as Prince Albert, its capital, which
was an old settlement, and now is a thriving little
town. This comparatively new country is gaining
a great reputation for sheep, cattle, and horse
raising. The land is fertile and well sheltered,
and settlers are flocking thither. Bryant's pro-
phecy is being rapidly fulfilled as the tide of human
life flows over the Great West—

These are the gardens of the Desert, these
The unshorn fields, boundless and beautiful,
For which the speech of England has no name —
The Prairies. I behold them for the first,
And my heart swells, while the dilated sight
Takes in the encircling vastness. Lo ! they stretch
In fairy undulations, far away,
As if the Ocean, in his gentlest swell,
Stood still, with all his rounded billows fixed
And motionless for ever. Motionless ?—
No !—they are all unchained again. The clouds
Sweep over with their shadows, and, beneath,
The surface rolls and fluctuates to the eye :
Dark hollows seem to glide along and chase
The sunny ridges.      *      *      *      *      *

Still, this great solitude is quick with life.
Myriads of insects, gaudy as the flowers
They flutter over, gentle quadrapeds
And birds—that scarce have learnt the fear of man—
Are here, and sliding reptiles of the ground
Startling'y beautiful. The graceful deer
Bounds to the wood at my approach. The bee —
A more adventurous colonist than man,
With whom he came across the Eastern deep—
Fills the savannahs with his murmurings,
And hides his sweets, as in the golden age,
Within the hollow oak. I listen long
To his domestic hum, and think I hear
The sound of that advancing multitude
Which soon shall fill these deserts. From the ground
Comes up the laugh of children, the soft voice
Of maidens, and the sweet and solemn hymn
Of Sabbath worshippers. The low of herds
Blends with the rustling of the heavy grain
Over the dark-brown furrows. All at once
A fresher wind sweeps by, and breaks my dream,
And I am in the wilderness alone.

Yes ! at the present day the "Church-going
bell" is heard in all the principal towns of the
North-West, and children are growing up in
health and beauty. Proceeding west from Regina,
the buildings visible from the Railway have more
of the ordinary farm look about them. Cattle
raising and wheat-growing appear to be conducted

in a systematic manner. The country soon becomes more broken, while numerous lakelets and ponds occupy the hollows. After the trees are left behind, the land seems more desolate, and is covered only with the thick buffalo grass. The occasional farms near the line appear to be prosperous, and large vegetables grow in the gardens around.

At Chaplin the Old Wives' Lakes, very large bodies of water, appear to the left of the road. They have no outlet, and consequently are alkaline. Skirting past these, we find ourselves in a veritable paradise for sportsmen. Some of the lakes are salt, but the most of them are clear and fresh. Here are myriads of wild ducks and geese, of plovers and snipe. These are all to be seen on the low ground, while "prairie chicken" are plentiful on the high ground, and antelopes numerous on the hills. The surface of the prairie is now marked in all directions with the old buffalo trails, and pitted with their "wallows." This noble denizen of the prairie is all but extinct. The great piles of white bleached bones, reared here and there along the line, show that these animals roamed in millions, and held undisputed sway over the entire west country before their extermination commenced with the appearance of the white man. At the stations along the route are to be seen many Indian squaws, with their papooses—not generally a very tidy-looking lot. They excite considerable curiosity among the passengers, and try to trade with them by exchanging pipes and trinkets for tobacco and silver. They are generally clothed in blankets of brilliant colours, mostly red. The Indians, notwithstanding the attention paid them by the Government in the way of provisions, &c., are gradually disappearing, and will soon become as extinct as the buffalo.

Before we arrive at Medicine Hat large herds of horses may be seen on either side of the line feeding on the rich grasses. Medicine Hat is a busy and important centre, with over 1000 inhabitants. There are several churches and other public buildings. This district, especially in the direction of Lethbridge, abounds in extensive coal mines, from which large supplies are daily shipped. After passing Medicine Hat, the high prairie is again marked deeply with the trails of buffaloes, and the round hollows in which they wallowed, while the plain is strewn over with their whitened skulls and bones. Farms appear at intervals, and large herds of cattle are seen grazing on some of the ranches. Reservoirs of natural gas have been discovered in this quarter. The gas is now being utilised for lighting and heating the station houses, and affording power for pumping water. The gas, when fully utilised, will prove an immense boon to the country.

At Crowfoot Station the first view of the Rocky Mountains, more than one hundred miles away, is obtained, and all the passengers are looking eagerly towards them. Soon there appears in the clear blue sky a glorious line of snow-capped peaks rising almost perpendicular from the plain, and stretching towards the western horizon as far as the eye can reach, forming apparently an impenetrable barrier. As the train approaches them peak seems to rise above peak, and dark belts of forest reaching near the snow line come in sight. The eternal glaciers and snow fields sparkle in the bright sunlight, while over the rolling tops of the foot-hills mountain passes cleft, as it were, into the very heart of the great mountains appear.

At Strathmore Station we are fairly into the country of the Backfeet, the most warlike and handsome of all the Indian tribes. They were once a terror and a dread, but now they live peacefully and quietly on a reservation near the line. The Bow River appears on the left hand side, and, immediately after the train crosses it by a steel bridge, the important city of Calgary is entered. The town of Calgary was only established in 1884, and already it has a population of 5000. As Winnipeg is the golden gate to the prairie on the east, so is Calgary the golden gate to the prairie on the west. It is the capital of the Province of Alberta, which now transports its immense resources of grain, cattle, sheep, and horses over the Rockies to Vancouver, whence they are shipped to all parts of the world. If Winnipeg is destined for a great future, so also is Calgary, as an agricultural, mineral, manufacturing, and distributing centre. It is beautifully situated on a hill-girt plateau, within sight of the snow-covered peaks of the Rockies, and is the centre of the extensive ranching country around. If its history is short it is yet one of solid and steady progress. There are fine hotels, beautiful churches, substantial banks, well-equipped schools, and all the other institutions and public buildings that go to make a great city, though it is yet only in its infancy. It boasts of two daily and three weekly newspapers. It is supplied with the telephone and electric light system. The Judge of the Supreme Court of Northern Alberta, the Superintendent of Dominion Mines, the Dominion Land Agent, the Registrar of land titles, and the Sheriff of Alberta all reside at Calgary. It is an important station of the North-West Mounted Police, and a post of the Hudson's Bay Company. In Calgary the enterprising ranchmen have a social club, conducted on a comfortable, if not a luxurious, scale. The majority of its members are connected with the best families in England and Scotland, and live here in a lordly style. Here they freely associate with men of humble origin, but pursuing the same calling as themselves. Thus the scions of noble houses and aristocratic families have here wisely and judiciously renounced all class distinctions. The advantages of such a social club, in such an important centre as Calgary, can scarcely be realised. It tends to make life, otherwise monotonous and dreary, extremely enjoyable and pleasant. An introduction to the club will prove most useful to the tourist. He will, at least, be most hospitably entertained, and it may probably lead to his receiving a cordial welcome to visit one of the extensive ranches in the neighbourhood. In the spring and autumn the ranchmen all join in a "round up." To gather and separate the animals, according to the brands of the different owners, is the glory of the "cowboy." To see the riders "cutting out" the animals from the common herd, lassoing and throwing them out in order that they may be marked with the owner's brand, or handling a drove of wild unbroken horses, is a scene not easily forgotten, and more than compensates for the fatigue and loss of time occasioned by a visit to the ranch. The ranchers are splendid riders, who love the ranch with its active life and unlimited opportunities for sport, as well as its entire disregard to the useless formalities to which the society of the old country necessarily clings. Some idea of the enormous extent of the ranching country may be formed from the fact that it measures over 90,000 square miles. The foot of the hills and the plains are carpeted with rich buffalo and other grasses, on which cattle and horses live, thrive, and fatten summer and winter without any shelter save what the nature of the undulating plains afford. The snow does not lie long, nor is it ever very deep. The ranchers cut and stack large quantities of hay in order to be prepared for emergencies. The pioneers of cattle ranching have devoted much valuable time and money to the introduction of well-bred horses and cattle. Thus a superior class of stock is always maintained on the best ranches.

Calgary forms a centre for the railway branch line that runs north to Edmonton and south to Fort M'Leod. Both branches throw open new and extensive districts, which comprise some of the richest and finest land in the North-West, and is now attracting many settlers, who, in comparison with the wooded part of Canada, find it extremely suitable and profitable for cultivation and the prosecution of mixed farming. Those who have been settled here for some time declare that the fertility of the land, opened up on either side by these two railway branch lines, is unsurpassed. Wonderful crops are produced, and the climate is suitable, thus rendering life here both enjoyable and prosperous. Marketing facilities are within reasonable distances. The producer being at no great distance from the railway, may have the result of his labours, whether in wheat or cattle, transferred by rail to the east or west coast for shipment. There is not a more excellent country in the new world than that around Calgary for mixed farming, and none with a more varied and charming scenery, or a more bracing and exhilarating climate. It abounds in all kinds of game for sport and horsemanship, and all that is capable of making life what it was originally intended to be.

Having now traversed the prairie from east to west, it may be stated generally that though apparently it is as level as a billiard table yet in reality it is a sloping country rising gradually towards the Rocky Mountains. Some of the buildings and homesteads are comparatively small, and sometimes do not add much to the natural beauty of the prairie. In many instances they resemble the small farmhouses of the home country. The prairie is specially fitted for wheat growing and catt'e raising. The inducements to grow wheat, which resulted generally in enormous returns, were such that it is not to be wondered at that settlers should largely avail themselves of it. It paid the producer well for a time, but soon the market became overstocked, and prices fell to such an extent that at present it scarcely pays the labour. The fall is due, not to want of richness in the soil, but to the overflow in the market. Threshing machines go about the country much in the same manner as at home, and charge from 1¼d to 1½d per bushel. The stubble is used for firing the engine. Some of the farmers club together and procure a threshing mill for themselves.

The prairie soil is the richest in the world. It has been discovered by analysis that the richness is due to the gathering of the droppings of myriad birds and animals that roamed undisturbed and at large over it for thousands of years, also to the ashes of prairie fires that swept over it from time to time, together with the decayed animal and vegetable matter which have accumulated for ages on the clay sub-soil. It is to this stored-up wealth in the soil that the settler is invited to look for a successful return to all his labours. The scruf is pretty tough, and a team of oxen will draw the plough steadier and for a longer period than a pair of horses. It is equally well adapted for raising potatoes and other vegetables, especially cabbage and cauliflower, without the assistance of anything in the shape of manure. The potato splits are laid in the furrow and covered over with the grass side of the sod. They are left in this state till ripe and ready for consumption. The yield from this simple process is marvellous, and the potatoes are not only numerous, but of a large size, dry, and mealy, so that they command the highest prices in the market. The native grasses are nutritive, and good for fattening cattle. The alternate sections on either side of the line for some twenty-four miles inland belong to the Canadian Pacific Railway Company, the others to the Government, and special facilities are offered by both to intending settlers. Rivers and lakes are numerous, and water may be found anywhere over the prairie by digging wells from sixteen to twenty-three feet deep. Wood for fuel can be procured at moderate rates, and extensive arrangements are in process for bringing coal at reasonable prices within easy reach. Manitoba and the western countries abound in good coal, one seam of which alone is two hundred miles broad. The tendency all over is to prosecute mixed farming as more profitable and reliable. The farmers rear horses, cattle, sheep, pigs, and poultry. Thus, when prices are low for one kind of stock or grain, they may be high in others. Mixed farming is also a protection against such disasters as were brought about by an over-production of grain. Such is the general character of the rolling country extending between Winnipeg and the Rocky Mountains, the area of which is over two hundred million acres, suitable more or less for agricultural purposes. It may be here stated that at the Chicago Exhibition Canada took all the leading prizes for dairy products, especially for cheese, and much more than her share for cattle, horses, and sheep of all kinds. This was a great surprise and disappointment to all, and especially to Americans, who have no love for the Dominion. But Canada has been prominently brought to the front by the exhibition awards, and is more than likely in the future to fully maintain her own in all the leading markets of the world. As to the general character of the climate, it is warm in summer and cold in winter. The seasons are subject to the climatic changes of all countries. The atmosphere is dry, clear, bright, free from damp, and extremely bracing. It is considered the healthiest climate in the world, pleasant to live in, free from malaria and other diseases, and especially so from rheumatics and chest complaints. Native horses and cattle thrive out even in winter. In spring rainfalls are frequent, but the summer and autumn are comparatively dry. There are, however, occasional frosts in August and September, and these the farmers have good reason to fear and dread. The intense frost and snow in the winter are almost necessary to secure a good crop in autumn. The ploughing, which is generally done towards the end of harvest, is left so for the winter, when the soil is broken and pulverised by the frost, without which the yield would not be nearly so heavy. The frost is thus of incalculable value to the success of the farmer.

Those interested will likely wish to know something of the school system of the Dominion, and let me refer to it here. The educational machinery in Canada is most complete, and all legislation, thereupon, is in the hands of the Government of the several provinces. They make admirable arrangements to meet all the requirements of the immediate province, with the result that no country can boast of the same extended educational facilities. In every township two sections, 640 acres each, of land are held in trust by the Dominion Government as school lands. The revenue derived from these, in the shape of feus, &c., augmented by Government grants, provide for the teaching staff. Wherever, therefore, a new settlement is started, and a school is required, the Government at once establishes one, free to all, provided that no less than ten children, from five to twenty years of age, are in the district. The poorest has equal rights and privileges with the richest. The schools are national, and do not recognise the religious differences of the people—unless in very special circumstances. Their superintendence is in the hands of the leading educators of the country, who are responsible for their being inspected twice a year by officials appointed for the purpose. The teachers must undergo a course of training, and receive a Government certificate, before they can be recognised as competent to teach. In addition to the public schools there are also collegiate institutes, maintained at the public expense, and free to all. When pupils have completed their education in the former they are prepared to enter the latter for training in the higher branches of study to qualify for entrance to the Normal Schools and Universities. The Professors and teachers are generally distinguished for their culture and ability. Private schools and academies are also to be found in the Dominion.

Sunday Schools are general throughout the country in connection with the different denominations. For the children's accommodation and convenience the churches are well equipped with halls, &c. But there are many union schools where the children of Christian parents of all creeds attend one Sunday School. The children have their picnics, trips, and soirees as at home. There is therefore ample, liberal, and free provision made for education. Wherever and whenever a settlement is started, a school is established free to all, and it is universally followed by the erection of a church or mission, so that the Sabbath bell is heard calling the people to the worship of the Father of all. In Canada the Sabbath is observed fully as well as in the old country, and the visitor is surprised at the stillness and peacefulness that reign on the hallowed morning, the devotional attitude of the people, and the regularity of their attendance at the churches. In this respect we may well take a leaf out of their book as regards church-going, Sabbath observance, Sabbath school organisations, and their educational system.

## Across the Rockies.

Leaving Calgary, and pursuing our journey westwards, the river terraces, foothills, and ranches, already described, are passed in rapid succession. Large herds of horses may be seen grazing on the valleys, cattle on the terraces, and flocks of sheep on the hill-tops, all affording a novel and interesting source of pleasure to the passengers. But surpassing in beauty and delight all the views of the low country is the first near prospect of the awe-inspiring glory of the snow-covered Rocky Mountains. After passing Cochrane Station, the line ascends to the top of the first terrace, and a splendid view is obtained to the left, where the foot hills are seen to rise in successive tiers of what seem to be sculptured heights up to the snow-line. " By-and-by the wide valleys change into broken ravines, and lo ! through an opening in the midst, made rosy with early sunlight, we see, far away up in the sky, its delicate pearly tip clear against the blue, a single snow-peak of the Rocky Mountains. . . . Our coarse natures cannot at first appreciate the exquisite aerial grace of that solitary peak that seems on its way to heaven ; but, as we look, gauzy mist passes over, and it has vanished." In approaching the Gap, the mountains appear impenetrable, and seem to form a barrier of grandeur and immensity. The bases of the lofty range, as seen by the approaching traveller, are deeply tinted in purple, their slopes tinged with white and gold, and their summits clothed with eternal snow, or shrouded in flying clouds of mist.

As the train enters fairly upon the great highway to the world-renowned Rockies, and nears the Gap station, the Bow River is seen issuing from the hills and rolling down through a narrow defile between two great mountain ranges. Then a magnificent spectacle bursts upon the view, where, on the left, the Three Sisters and Wind Mountains are seen to tower majestically aloft as if they were seeking to lose themselves in heaven. The contrast between these and the ranges farther on is remarkable. To the right are fantastically broken and castellated heights, down whose sides dash foaming cascades, some of them several thousand feet in height. On the left again, as we advance, tremendous snow-covered peaks, penetrated by deep-cut recesses, are seen, in which the light and shadow falling upon the glittering snow makes them often assume a gorgeous colouring of varying rainbow hues. Glorious glimpses of glaciers and other strange sights may be caught, and now and again mountain sheep and wild goats appear leisurely grazing on the rugged cliffs above. The mountains visible are tremendous uplifts of stratified rocks of the Devonian and Carboniferous strata, which have burst up through the crust of the earth, and have heaved themselves aloft. Some sections, miles and miles broad and thousands of feet thick, have been forced straight upwards, so that their strata continues to rise in the same direction as it was originally; others are tossed on edge, and lie in a steeply slanting position; other sections look as if they had been bent by a terrible side pressure, but all have been broken down and worn away more or less, so that now they remain colossal fragments of the first tremendous upheavals. The disturbed statification may be noticed on the face of the cliffs by the lines of trees struggling for a scanty foothold, or by the ledges that retained the snows which have vanished from the place in close proximity. The scenery in all directions is splendid; it is terrific in its grandeur, and baffles all description.

At Anthracite Station, overshadowed by the Cascade Mountains, are large coal mines yielding the best quality. Lady Macdonald thus describes the outlook—"Here the pass we are travelling through has narrowed suddenly to four miles, and, as mists float upwards and away, we see great masses of scarred rock rising on each side—ranges towering one above the other. Very striking and magnificent grows the prospect as we penetrate into the mountains at last, each curve of the line bringing fresh vistas of endless peaks rolling away before and around us, all tinted rose, blush-pink, and silver, as the sun lights their snowy tips. Every turn becomes a fresh mystery, for some huge mountain seems to stand right across our way, barring it for miles, with a stern face frowning down upon us ; and yet a few minutes later we find the giant has been encircled and conquered, and soon lies far away in another direction."

Banff Station, situated in the midst of impressive mountain scenery, is soon reached.

## Banff.

has already earned a world-wide reputation from its hot and sulphurous springs, which, on account of their curative qualities, are attracting thousands of tourists from all parts of the world. For miles around the Canadian Government have reserved this supremely beautiful country as a national park, in the centre of which a commodious and luxuriously appointed hotel has been erected by the Canadian Pacific Railway Company for the accommodation of the tourists who flock thither. The mountain, forest, valley, and river scenery within sight of the hotel is without rival. Bridle paths and well-made carriage roads lead in all directions. The impression left by the grand and varied scenery that appears all round can never be erased from the memory. The hotel is well fitted up with baths, and near it is a circular pavilion for resting, smoking, &c. The springs have been vastly improved by the Government, and attendants are placed by it in charge of all the bathing houses. At no great distance from the village of Banff is a hot circular pool covered by a dome-roofed cave with a hole on the top, which admits sufficient light, while in the near vicinity is an open basin of warm sulphurous water. Banff is a famous centre for mountain-climbing and for excursions on river and lake, in which abundance of trout are to be found. On the surrounding heights are wild sheep, goats, and other animals, as well as game of various kinds. Resuming our journey west, the train passes through a thickly-wooded valley and skirts Vermillion Lakes, while in front are enormous snow and ice ledges hanging to the mountains, or resting on the deep crevices. After passing Castle Mountain and Eldon Stations the mountains on either side look grand and bold in the extreme. The loftiest and grandest in the whole panorama of vision is the helmet-shaped mount called Lefroy. The next station is Laggan, thirty-four miles west of Banff. This is the depôt for the Lakes in the Clouds, which are largely frequented by tourists. The lakes should by all means be visited, for they are extremely interesting and picturesque. Horses and vehicles are in attendance at all the trains to convey travellers to a small chalet, where lunch may be taken and a bed for the night may also be had. The chalet is situated on the margin of Lake Louise. The first of the great glaciers can be seen from it lying on the side of the mountain some 1300 feet above the level where we now stand. Stephen Station is the next halting-place. It is 5296 feet above sea level, and is the summit station of the Rocky Mountains, though by no means the summit of the mountains, for the snow-covered mountains tower from 5000 to 8000 feet above the level of this station. From this the train rapidly descends, passing some beautiful emerald lakes, and then a tortuous gorge deeply cut in the rocks is crossed. Here the water is seen foaming far below and dashing down the gorge with enormous force. This canyon is known as Wapta, or Kicking Horse Pass. The scenery here I can only describe as terrible. The line clings fast to the mountain side, and winds its way down towards the valley. Away to the north glacier-bound peaks are visible, and almost overhead is a glacier shining like green ice, some 800 feet in thickness, and gradually falling over a sheer precipice of dizzy height. The line still continues to follow the river, crossing and recrossing deep gorges, gliding over rocky spurs, and passing babbling brooks, beautiful lakelets, and splendid forests. Soon a sawmill, a slate quarry, and other signs of industry are seen, and as quickly left behind ; and we plunge through a tremendous gorge whose frowning cliffs are 1000 feet high and seem to overhang the boiling, roaring stream at the base. Through this awful chasm the railway and the river struggle together, "the former crossing from side to side to ledges cut out of the solid rock and twisting and turning in every direction, and every minute or two plunging through projecting angles of rock which seem to close the way. With the towering cliffs almost shutting out the sunlight, and the roar of the river and the train increased an hundredfold by the echoing walls, the passage of this terrible gorge will never be forgotten." It then suddenly widens out, and there stand boldly in front, against the clear blue sky, a jagged line of snow-clad peaks of new colours and various forms. In the dense forest-clad valley which intervenes flows the noble Columbia river. These are the famous Selkirk Mountains, differing widely in aspect, but all indescribably grand. At last we reach Golden Station. Golden is a mining town built on the bank of the Columbia at the mouth of the Wapta. Gold and silver mines are worked with considerable success in the near vicinity. From this place a steamer sails up the Columbia to the lakes at the head of the river. It is a favourite trip for sportsmen, and the scenery all along is most beautiful.

Leaving Golden the train sweeps through a deep narrow gorge, from which it emerges at Beavermouth, and enters the Selkirks through the gate of Beaver river. Here the passage is so narrow that a felled tree can be utilised to bridge it over, and the river makes a final mad plunge into the Columbia. The train now commences to climb the shoulder of the Selkirks, through dense forests of enormous trees, till it arrives at the summit. Here is a broad, level area shut in by mountain monarchs, held in the deadly grasp of the eternal glaciers. Between here and Bear Creek the snow in the winter occasioned the greatest dangers to the railway, but these difficulties were completely overcome by the construction of sheds or tunnels of heavy timber fitted and bolted into the mountain side in such a manner as to bid defiance to the most terrific avalanche. These tunnels, as you can well suppose, were erected at great expense.

Descending from the summit of the Selkirks and passing through scenery awful and overpowering in its grandeur, we at last arrive at Glacier House, at the foot of Sir Donald, the grandest of the Selkirk peaks, shooting up nearly 8000 feet, like a pyramid of naked rock. This majestic and glorious mountain was called after Sir Donald Smith, one of the chief promoters of the Canadian

Pacific Railway. The hotel at Glacier House has been erected by the Railway Company, is very comfortable, and tourists would find a couple of days' stay here to be most interesting and delightful. Facilities are afforded for visiting the glaciers around, especially the great glacier, and for exploring the mountains, as well as for hunting bears, goats, and other wild animals, or having some sport amongst the game, which is here very abundant. The Illicilliwaet, with its pea-green-coloured waters from the glaciers, can be seen from here. Resuming our journey for hours, the train plunges through marvellous scenery, precipitous gorges, and again crosses the Columbia River. It is wider and deeper here, and is navigated by comfortable steamers southward for about 200 miles.

Ravelstoke, on the bank of the Columbia, which has made a great detour round the north-eastern extremity of the Selkirks, looks splendid. The Kootenay district, which is now entered, abounds in gold, silver, and copper mines, and is within easy reach by rail or steamer. The lake and mountain scenery in this part of the country is superb. Pursuing our journey westward, we are next confronted by the Gold Range, a grand series of snow-clad peaks, broken across by a deep ravine, through which the train plunges, till a sudden flash of light indicates that it has emerged from the dark, precipitous pass. Then many lakes come in sight, but, the view being intercepted by the abruptly-rising mountains, they are lost again in a few minutes.

Okanagan Lake district is not far distant from this part. As we proceed, the valley of the South Thompson River is soon reached, and, from what I saw, it appears to be largely taken up with cattle-ranching and farming. At Craigellachie the last spike in the Canadian Pacific Railway was driven in on 7th November, 1885 ; the rails from east and west meet here. Then we sweep into Kamloops, the most important town in the interior of British Columbia, with over 2000 of a population. The district is famous for ranching and fruit-growing, and abounds in minerals. Leaving Kamloops behind, the train shoots through tunnel after tunnel, with scarred and rugged mountains frowning down upon it, and far below a foaming river, till, quickly crossing the deep, dark gorge of the Fraser River on a steel bridge, which looks like a fairy bridge hung in mid-air, it rushes through a tunnel and enters the famous Fraser Canyon. The scenery now on all hands is grand and wild. Through this gorge, so narrow and deep that the rays of the sun seldom or never penetrate its dark recesses, the fierce and foaming waters of the noble river plough their mighty way. The railway line is stuck into the face of the tremendous cliffs, at a height of several hundred feet above the angry, whirling waters. A safe road is here made for the train, which sweeps now over terrible chasms by means of tall and airy-looking viaducts, and now through tunnels cut in the overhanging rocks ; and all along the passengers are being constantly deafened by the roar of the waters below. Yet, notwithstanding the apparently dangerous and bewildering situation, there is a feeling of entire safety, and the scene, which is altogether fascinating by reason of its terror, is very regretfully left behind as we enter Yale.

Yale has a population of 1500. The ranchers and miners of the district receive their outfittings from the town, which is the head of the navigation of the Fraser River. Chinamen may be seen washing gold on the sand-bars, with their boat high and dry on the shore beside them. This operation is generally carried on by two men. The one is in charge of the gold-washing machine at the water edge, the other carries from a short distance quantities of sand and rubble to supply the machine, so to speak. The work is carried on all day, from sunrise till dusk, when the few grains they may have succeeded in collecting is carried safely home with them in the boat. Their dwellings are visible on the opposite bank, and their Joss House also is conspicuous in the hamlet. Indians may be seen herding cattle in the meadows or fishing for salmon on the river. This last operation is also carried on by two men. The one is provided with a bag net fixed to a loop of wood resembling a snow-shoe in shape, and that is firmly attached to a long pole. The other stands on a cliff above ready to receive and despatch the fish. Armed with this long pole and net the fisher takes his stand on a ledge of rock near an eddy formed by an outlying rock or boulder, and so far up stream as he can reach he lets the net drop into the water, and, with a quick sweep down past where he stands, he lifts it out of the water. If a fish appears in the net, he holds it up to the man above, who takes it out, kills, and splits it. An enormous quantity of salmon is caught in this way. After being split up, they are hung to dry in rows on long poles, somewhat similar to those used at home for drying nets, but not so high. Thus they are dried and cured in the open air, though in some cases a light roof is thrown over the drying-poles. This cured salmon is the provision made by the Indian for his winter store. His " bread and water " may fail him, but assuredly his fish and water never fail him. As the seasons come round, so does the rush of salmon in the river, and that in such enormous shoals that they may even be seen sometimes to crush each other in large numbers out of the water on to the dry bank. The visitor will also be interested in the curious looking graveyards of the Indians, neatly enclosed and decorated with banners, streamers, &c., which are to be seen along the line now and again. Chinese and Indian villages are passed in close succession.

Mount Baker, a gleaming white cone, rising some 13,000 feet above the railway level, stands proudly towards the south. As the valley widens out, farms and orchards are constantly within sight ; and, as we approach the coast, we find the climate becomes as mild as that of the south of England, but with more sunshine. The glimpses which we get of the Fraser river show that it has now become smooth and glassy, with an occasional steamer plying upon it, while in many places its waters are dotted with Indian canoes engaged in salmon catching. Large cannaries are erected along its banks. In these many are employed in preparing the salmon for preservation in tins, which are despatched to all the leading markets of the world. After passing through a forest of huge trees, some 300 feet high and twelve or more feet in diameter, we arrive at the tide-waters of the Pacific at the eastern extremity of Burrard Inlet. Sweeping down the shore of this mountain-girt inlet, our train rolls into Vancouver Station, the western terminus of the Canadian Pacific Railway.

# Vancouver.

This beautiful town has a population of over 20,000, and bids well to become one of the most famous cities in America. As recently as 1886 the site on which it stands was covered with dense forests. In June of the same year a terrible and destructive fire swept every house in the old town, with one exception, out of existence. The buildings were all of wood, but ere the embers of the conflagration died out materials for the reconstruction of the buildings were on their way, and the old erections were replaced by grand and substantial blocks of stone, brick, and iron. The large transportation interests, which were established at Vancouver in 1887, gave the town such a tremendous impetus that most of the timber was cleared away, broad streets were formed, and electric cars placed upon them. The Hotel Vancouver for comfort, luxury, and excellence of service is among the best on the continent, while the Opera House is unsurpassed by any outside New York. There are churches, schools, hospitals, and all the other public buildings that are the precursors of a great commercial centre. The whole town is laid out on a magnificent scale. It is surrounded by a country of rare beauty, enjoying a climate milder and less varying than that of the south of England. To the north, close at hand, are the Cascade Mountains; to the west over the channel are the mountains of Vancouver Island; to the south-west the Olympics, and towards the south-east the majestic Mount Baker. The town is thus protected on every side, while the fresh sea breeze from the Straits of Georgia is most enjoyable. The situation as regards picturesqueness, harbour facilities, commercial advantages, and natural drainage is perfect. It has splendid and inexhaustible water supply brought in pipes laid under the inlet from a mountain stream on the opposite side. There are very extensive wharves, warehouses, and a commodious harbour. But in addition to the great transportation of the Canadian Pacific Railway Company by land, the same enterprising Company has established a line of steamers between Vancouver, Japan, and China. These are magnificent steel ships designed for the trade, and fitted up in a most luxurious style. They are so constructed that, in case of emergency, they can readily be converted on the shortest of notice into war cruisers. The route thus opened up shortens the journey to the places indicated by three weeks. There are daily steamers to Victoria and connection is made with all Puget Sound ports, Portland, and San-Francisco by land and sea, and new systems are in operation to bring Vancouver into even closer connection with all the leading towns on the Pacific Coast. The country extending towards the Fraser river has splendid farms and is specially adapted for fruit growing. The sport is unlimited by sea and land, while coal is supplied in abundance from across the Sound. The progress and prosperity of Vancouver is beyond the limits of speculation. The natural position it occupies, and the natural facilities it enjoys, are bound to make it, what it is destined to be, one of the leading towns of the world.

Vancouver is connected with New Westminster by electric cars. This thriving and flourishing little town has over 8000 of a population. It was founded by Colonel Moody during the gold excitement in 1858, and now has many new and beautiful buildings. It is the headquarters of the salmon-canning industry, and the importance of the trade may be gathered from the fact that from five to eight thousand men are employed at it during the fishing season. The agricultural interests of the district are coming rapidly to the front and giving the city additional stability. There is also an extensive lumber trade. The Provincial Penitentiary and Insane Asylum are at New Westminster. These establishments are conducted in first-class style, and are under the general superintendence of Dr Bentley, who has thrown his whole heart and soul into the work, with the result that he has earned for himself a wide reputation and the respect and confidence of all who come in contact with him. The religious oversight of the establishment is in the hands of the venerable Archdeacon Woods, a true specimen of what a man of his dignity and position should be. The noble Fraser River sweeps majestically past in front of the town, and the outlook on mountain, valley, wood, and forest is exquisite.

Returning from New Westminster to Vancouver, and going on board one of the new Clyde-built steamers, a five-hours' sail through a most lovely archipelago, with scenery of the grandest description spreading in every direction brings us to

## Victoria,

the capital of British Columbia. It has a population of over 20,000, and is beautifully situated at the southern extremity of Vancouver Island, which is 300 miles long, with an average of 50 miles broad. Originally a stockaded post of the Hudson's Bay Company, it received a special impetus in 1858, when the discovery of gold on the mainland brought a rush of miners from the south by vessels to Victoria, from which they crossed the channel in canoes. The declivity on which the city is built rises gradually from an arm of the sea, which forms a splendid harbour. The harbour is well protected by the formation of the land, and is capable of accommodating and sheltering in the roughest weather the largest vessels and steamers that sail the Pacific Ocean. There are no dangerous rocks at the entrance, while the wharves are excellent, with sufficient water depth to enable ships of any size to come alongside. The wharves as well as the town are lighted by electricity. On landing the tourist is struck with the purely English character of the city and its inhabitants.

The business streets of Victoria are wide and handsome, regard being always had not, if possible, to concentrate the business life of the town into one street, as is common in many cities. It is worthy of notice that nine-tenths of the city residents own their own houses, and, if engaged in business, their business property as well. The wealthiest citizens have erected magnificent homes on the heights around in the near vicinity. In the town are fine blocks and beautiful private residences. The churches show great architectural taste and beauty, as do also the colleges, schools, hospitals, hotels, and other public establishments. There are two excellent clubs where accredited strangers are hospitably entertained by the Victorians. Manufacturing industries are yearly growing in extent and importance. There are mills of every description, iron works surpassed only by those of San Francisco, and half-a-dozen breweries.

Socially, Victoria offers attractions which can scarcely b, excelled. Here are the Parliament Buildings, Courts, and Government Offices of the Province, as well as the headquarters of Her Majesty's fleet in the North Pacific. The naval officers are always available for festivities, and their presence adds to the social pleasures of the city. The citizens are highly cultured, due no doubt to the splendid advantages for education and refinement afforded by the town.

There are beautiful drives in the neighbourhood, and the natives are truly proud of Beacon Hill Park. It consists of several hundred acres, intersected with carriage drives lined with oak trees in some parts and closely wooded in others. In the park are a few small lakes, on which wild fowl may be seen, while the bear pit and deer pen present some fine native specimens. A part of the park is utilized as a recreation ground for the city, cricket, football, baseball, lacrosse, and such games being here freely indulged in. On Sunday afternoon the people turn-out to hear the band, when the park presents a gay and fashionable appearance.

Victoria transacts an enormous business with the mainland, and is the main centre for the salmon fishing, which utilizes a special fleet of sailing vessels alone. It is also a celebrated centre for the seal industry, and for all the mines on the island—gold, silver, coal, and quicksilver are all to be found. Farming and other branches of agriculture, such as hock raising, fruit growing, sheep and cattle rearing, are prosecuted with considerable success, but the soil and climate are more adapted for fruit than for agriculture. A railway line extends north-east to Nanaimo, celebrated for its coal mines, while the electric car goes to Esquimault, where the finest harbour in the island is, and where the British warships usually lie. The naval yard and dry dock—the latter capable of accommodating the largest ships that ride the seas—should be inspected. The scenery about the harbour is very beautiful. The climate compares favourably with that of California or the south of England. The summer heat is softened by the breezes from the sea, while the hottest days are followed by cool and pleasant evenings. Victoria is a most picturesque and interesting city. Its

scenic splendours are extensive, varied, and unrivalled. Across the Sound is the Olympic Range,
with its glittering snow-capped and even peaks extending towards the west of Washington State ;
to the east beyond Puget Sound is the Cascade
Mountain range with its forest-clad foothills.
There is Mount Rainier, the pride and glory of
Washington, and there is Mount Baker with its
gleaming mantle of eternal snow. To the north
are the great ranges of British Columbia with their
white peaks, the Selkirks, and the Fraser, and the
Georgian Straits, picturesquely dotted with innumerable islands, all comprehended in one sweep,
and forming an unique panorama.

No tourist should fail to make the round trip
from Victoria to Tacoma and Seattle by Puget
Sound. It is scarcely possible to conceive a more
charming and interesting sail than that on one of
the beautiful and well-appointed steamers placed
on the route.

British Columbia affords little scope for
settlers as compared with the north-west, and
for those desirous of taking possession,
the facilities afforded to intending emigrants are
all that could be desired. Free grants of one
quarter-section (160 acres) of surveyed agricultural
lands may be obtained by any person who is the
sole head of a family, or by any male who has attained the age of 18 years on application to the
local agent of Dominion Lands for the district
in which the parcel applied for is situated,
and on payment of an office fee of $10.
The only charge for a homestead of this
size is the entrance fee of ten dollars or £2.
No farm servant goes to Canada with the intention
of continuing to be merely a servant. If he be a
good worker, economical and steady in his habits,
possessed of some energy and shrewdness, he is
bound to become his own master in a few years.
A man of this stamp should take up a quarter
section, or 160 acres of land, alongside a section
already under cultivation, to the owner of which
he should engage himself on condition that he
should be allowed time, and possibly assistance, to
break and cultivate so many acres of his own
newly acquired land while so employed. He thus
learns how to work the soil and adapt himself to
the methods of the country. A man who starts on
this principle is certain of success. Small farmers

or farm labourers, and such as have been accustomed to agricultural work, with half grown-up families, able and determined to work honestly, are specially suitable for emigration, and, after the trouble and inconvenience of settling are got over, may be almost guaranteed to prosper on a mixed farm in the North-West. Young men with a taste for agricultural labour, horse and cattle breeding, possessed of some means, with shrewd and business habits, can scarcely fail to prosper. But no man should invest his money till he is sure of his ground and knows how to work the land. Ample information of the minutest description can be supplied to any intending settler, *free* of charge, by any of the agents. There is thus no reason whatever why he should not fully satisfy himself before leaving home as to the land most suitable for him, the nature of the climate of the district, the convenience of water supply, of material for building, of feul, of market, of railway station, &c., &c. All this information it is important to know at the outset, and can be provided. The object of the Government is not to disappoint settlers after arrival, but to make them as comfortable as possible in order that they may induce more of their friends to follow them into a wider sphere where there are better prospects of success than the limitations of the old country can afford. But there are other classes of people that it would be utterly wrong to advise to go to Canada, for example, those who have not been more or less accustomed to agricultural labour, those who have been brought up to idle lives in our large cities and towns and who have never followed any regular occupation. These without means will meet with little or no encouragement whatever. Neither will those ever succeed who are not prepared for hard work, or who think that they can live there with their hands in their pockets. Such people will be of no use out there, and they tend to give a bad name to the country of their adoption. There is no country in the world that offers better facilities and fairer prospects of success than the North-West of Canada, with its indescribable scenery, unlimited sport, land of the most fertile description, and capable of accommodating and providing in abundance for millions of our race—a place where they can acquire possessions, freedom, and liberty that is quite unknown in the mother country. Canada altogether is a grand country to fight and struggle in, with the perfect assurance that so long as a man works faithfully, and acts honourably, he will never lack his daily bread, the comforts of life, and the freedom to think and to act as his conscience and his will dictate.

Of the remainder of my tour in America, I have notes sufficiently full for even more elaborate descriptions than the preceding, but, in presence of other matters of more imperative claims upon my time, they shall have to remain in abeyance meanwhile. Proceeding south from Victoria to California, San Francisco was entered by the "Golden Gate," and, under the escort of a private detective, a midnight round was accomplished through China-town, the opium dens, the theatre, and Joss House. After seeing the wonderful sights of the great metropolis some fruit and grain ranches of enormous extent were visited, as was also a gold mine in operation. Then the Sierra Mountains were crossed to Salt Lake City—the famous Mormon town—with its beautiful tabernacle, splendid organ, excellent choir of over 600 members, and crowded congregation of from 7000 to 8000 people. It is said to be the largest and the best attended church in the States. Proceeding by stages east to Colorado Springs and Mainton, near the Garden of the Gods, Pike's Peak, 14,447 feet high was ascended by the highest railway in the world. Thence to Denver, continuing east to Chicago, where ten days were spent at the World's Fair, which looked more like a lovely little town than an exhibition. The buildings, which were nearly all white, were simply magnificent, and shone in the bright sun after a shower of rain like polished marble. The "big show" was a sight and an experience that can never be forgotten by all who were fortunate enough to see it. The next important town arrived at was Washington, the capital of America. It is laid out on a magnificent scale with lovely avenues, fine broad streets, splendid car system, substantial blocks and beautiful Government buildings, standing on a high hill, and commanding a grand view. I left Washington for Philadelphia, Baltimore, and New York, where the most of a week was spent, and finished off by visiting the Emigrants' Island and ascending the Statue of Liberty in the harbour before going on board the City of Rome direct for Glasgow, where I arrived on the 22d October, 1893, after traversing over 16,000 miles by land and water.